The Enlargement
of the European Union

Contemporary European Studies, 1

Series Editor
Clive Archer

The Enlargement of the European Union

Graham Avery & Fraser Cameron

Sheffield
Academic Press

First published by Sheffield Academic Press 1998
Reprinted 1999, 2001

Copyright © 1998, 1999, 2001 Sheffield Academic Press

Published by
Sheffield Academic Press Ltd
Mansion House
19 Kingfield Road
Sheffield S11 9AS
England

Typeset by Sheffield Academic Press
and
Printed on acid-free paper in Great Britain
by Cromwell Press
Trowbridge, Wiltshire

British Library Cataloguing in Publication Data

A catalogue record for this book is available
from the British Library

ISBN 1-85075-853-0

Contents

Series Foreword

This is the first publication in a new series—*Contemporary European Studies*—resulting from collaboration between the Sheffield Academic Press and the University Association for Contemporary European Studies (UACES).

For over 25 years UACES has been the lead organization in bringing together academics and practitioners concerned with the study of contemporary Europe. The main emphasis of the Association's work has been in the sphere of European integration and, increasingly, has been concerned with the institutions and activities of the European Union. This series will reflect those interests, but will also respond to the needs of those studying contemporary Europe by providing authoritative texts dealing with a wide range of issues, with the emphasis on the European Union. As series editor, I have tried to produce a balance in the three to four publications each year which, from now on, will be appearing under the title of *Contemporary European Studies*, so that theoretical and policy issues are covered and, in the case of the European Union, external relations are included as well as the internal concerns of the EU. It was also one of the intentions of the series to include promising younger authors—as well as some more experienced hands—in the list of contributors, and this concern will be reflected in our annual list of publications.

Graham Avery and Fraser Cameron, the authors of this vanguard publication for the *Contemporary European Studies* series, are members of the European Commission team that has been dealing with the 'millennial' enlargement of the European Union and are thus well placed to produce an authoritative text on the issue. Their contribution is timely in its subject matter and in appearing during a British presidency of the European Council.

In the production of this book, I am grateful to Hans van den Broek, the European Commissioner responsible for enlargement, for kindly agreeing to provide a Foreword; to Professor Stephen George, Professor Michael Smith and Professor William Paterson—the present and previous two past chairmen of UACES—for their support for the series; and to Mrs Jean Allen of Sheffield Academic Press for her ready assistance in bringing the series to fruition.

Clive Archer
Series Editor

Foreword

Enlargement of the European Union to include the countries of central and eastern Europe is one of the most important political and economic issues on today's international agenda. It is a process that began with the political upheavals almost a decade ago and will not end until the reunification of Europe is complete.

An enlarged EU will bring increased security, stability and prosperity to Europe. Never before has the Union envisaged enlargement on such a scale. Its population—currently some 370 million—will increase by more than 100 million. The next enlargement will clearly present many challenges and the Union will have to find new approaches and new solutions, while strengthening the existing system. If the EU is to maintain its coherence and effectiveness then it needs to ensure that new members are ready to take on all the obligations of membership.

As the Commissioner responsible for central and eastern Europe, I welcome the decisions of the European Council in December 1977 on enlargment, which largely reflect the Commission's recommendations, put forward in its Agenda 2000 report. The reinforced pre-accession strategy will apply to all candidates demonstrating the Union's inclusive approach to enlargement. With a doubling of financial assistance, individual accession partnerships with all candidates, an annual review mechanism, and a European Conference involving all candidates and Member States, the Union has established a comprehensive set of policies to prepare the next enlargement.

This book provides a valuable overview of the Union's relations with the central and eastern European countries and the preparation for enlargement. I commend it to a wide readership.

Hans van den Broek

Abbreviations

BSEC	Black Sea Economic Corporation
CAP	Common Agricultural Policy
CEECs	Central and Eastern European Countries
CEFTA	Central European Free Trade Area
CEI	Central European Initiative
CEPR	Centre for European Policy Research
CEPS	Centre for European Policy Studies
CER	Centre for European Reform
CFE	Conventional Armed Forces in Europe
CFP	Common Fisheries Policy
CFSP	Common Foreign and Security Policy
CIS	Commonwealth of Independent States
CJTF	Combined Joint Task Force
CMEA	Council for Mutual Economic Assistance
COREPER	Committee of Permanent Representatives
EAPC	Euro-Atlantic Partnership Council
EBRD	European Bank for Reconstruction and Development
EC	European Community
ECOFIN	Economic and finance ministers Council
ECU	European currency unit
EEC	European Economic Community
EFTA	European Free Trade Association
EIB	European Investment Bank
EMU	Economic and Monetary Union
EPC	European Political Cooperation
ESDI	European Security and Defence Identity
EU	European Union
FDI	Foreign Direct Investment
FYROM	Former Yugoslav Republic of Macedonia
GDP	gross domestic product
IGC	Intergovernmental Conference
IMF	International Monetary Fund
JHA	Justice and home affairs
NACC	North Atlantic Cooperation Council

NATO	North Atlantic Treaty Organization
NIS	Newly Independent States
OECD	Organization for Economic Cooperation and Development
OSCE	Organization for Security and Cooperation in Europe
PCA	Partnership and Cooperation Agreement
PfP	Partnership for Peace
Phare	Pologne, Hongrie: assistance à la reconstruction economique (Poland, Hungary: assistance for economic reconstruction)
PJC	Permanent Joint Council
RIIA	Royal Institute of International Affairs
SEI	Sussex European Institute
SMEs	Small and Medium-sized Enterprises
TAIEX	Technical Assistance Information Exchange Office
TENs	trans-European Networks
UACES	University Association for Contemporary European Studies
UK	United Kingdom
US	United States
WEU	Western European Union
WTO	Warsaw Treaty Organization
WTO	World Trade Organization

Introduction

Since the publication of our book *The Enlargement of the European Union* in 1998, much has happened in the EU enlargement process.

Accession negotiations were opened with Hungary, Poland, Estonia, the Czech Republic, Slovenia and Cyprus in March 1998, and with Romania, Slovakia, Latvia, Lithuania, Bulgaria and Malta in February 2000. In the negotiations, most of the 31 chapters have been opened with the applicant countries, and a number of them have been provisionally closed. Turkey's inclusion in the overall accession process has been confirmed. The EU institutions have expressed the hope that the first accessions will take place in time for the new member states to participate in the elections for the European Parliament in 2004.

Taking account of this progress, we believe that our survey of the background, procedures and implications of this enlargement—the most important that the EU has undertaken—remains useful for readers in universities, the public administration and for members of the general public interested in EU affairs.

Graham Avery   *Fraser Cameron*
Brussels   Washington D.C.
March 2001

The idea for this book arose out of the numerous demands made on the authors to explain the European Union's plans to extend to include the central and eastern Europe countries (CEECs). There has been enormous interest from academics, journalists, researchers and others in the process of enlargement. We felt, therefore, that it would be useful to put together some of the most important documentation concerning EU and NATO enlargement, and to provide a commentary on the major issues. Our views are, of course, personal and are not official positions of the European Commission.

Chapter 1 reviews the relationship between the European Union (EU) and the CEECs from the end of the Cold War to the pre-accession strategy. Chapter 2 examines the enlargement process itself, referring to the timing and complexity of previous enlargements. Chapter 3 examines how the Commission made its Opinions on the central and eastern European applicant countries (Hungary, Poland, Romania, Slovakia, Latvia, Estonia, Lithuania, Bulgaria, the Czech Republic, Slovenia) and its recommendations concerning the opening of accession negotiations. Chapter 4 summarizes the Opinions, and Chapter 5 covers the Mediterranean dimension, including the Opinions of Turkey, Cyprus and Malta. Chapter 6 provides an overview of Agenda 2000 and Chapter 7 considers the reactions to Agenda 2000 in the institutions, in the Member States and in the candidate countries. Chapter 8 explores the impact of enlargement on the Union itself, and the geopolitical implications of enlargement, with the emphasis on the EU's most immediate neighbours. Chapter 9 reviews the parallel but separate process of NATO enlargement. Chapter 10 is the Conclusion. There are also a chronology and bibliography.

In preparation of this book, we would like to thank numerous colleagues in the Commission for their encouragement and support. The book would not have been possible without the efforts of Solveig Jaspert to prepare the text and documents in a readable fashion. Needless to say, any errors and omissions remain the responsibility of the authors.

Graham Avery   *Fraser Cameron*
Brussels
December 1997

1 |

Europe after the End of the Cold War

The advent to power of Mikhail Gorbachev in 1985 and his subsequent pursuit of 'perestroika' and 'glasnost' paved the way for the end of the Cold War, the most dramatic manifestation of which was the fall of the Berlin Wall in November 1989. During the Cold War, the population of the Central and Eastern European Countries (CEECs) had been led to believe by Western leaders that once the yoke of Communism had been thrown off they would be welcomed back into the mainstream of European development. For most people this meant membership of the EU and NATO.[1]

The EU's initial reaction to the collapse of Communism was one of general satisfaction and an immediate offer of financial assistance. At the G7 summit in Paris in 1989 Western leaders agreed on a technical assistance programme which would be coordinated by the European Commission. This programme, originally baptized Phare (Poland and Hungary—Assistance for economic reconstruction) was soon extended to other countries in the region. Whilst grateful for this assistance, the new reform leaderships in the CEECs were determined to push for full EU membership as swiftly as possible. The EU, however, had other priorities. It was involved both in the internal transformation resulting in the Treaty of Maastricht (1992) and the management of an extremely fluid and dangerous external situation, including the break-up of the Soviet Union, the unification of Germany, the outbreak of conflict in former Yugoslavia, and the Gulf War.

Some CEECs (Poland and Hungary) moved more rapidly than others to adopt reform policies. Others (the Baltic states) struggled to liberate themselves from the former Soviet Union. Some (Slovenia) were caught up in new conflicts. In this rapidly changing situation, there was

---

1.   Timothy Garton Ash, *In Europe's Name, Germany and the Divided Continent* (London: Jonathan Cape, 1993) provides a good overview of the end of the Cold War.

little alternative for the EU but to adopt ad hoc policies towards individual countries based on the level of their political and economic reforms. Initially trade and cooperation agreements were signed with the more advanced countries but these were soon superseded by association or 'Europe' agreements, and later a coherent preaccession strategy was developed to prepare the CEECs for membership of the Union. To a large extent the countries with Europe Agreements chose themselves, by indicating their wish for full membership of the EU. The first group were the Visegrad countries (Poland, Hungary, Czechoslovakia), followed by Bulgaria, Romania, the Baltic states and Slovenia.

The Europe Agreement negotiations in 1991 proved the first major test of relations between the EU and the CEECs. The Agreements are based on Article 238 of the EC Treaty, which means that they are 'mixed' agreements, necessitating ratification by the Community and Member States. All Europe Agreements follow a similar pattern in terms of structure and content providing for cooperation in political, economic, trade, cultural and other areas such as competition and state aids, and approximation of laws. There is provision for regular meetings at different levels, for example ministerial, senior official, and parliamentarian, to discuss issues of common concern. The Agreements further aim at establishing a free trade area, as well as preferential treatment of trade in agricultural products including those already processed; free trade in many services; national treatment for establishment and operation of enterprises; national treatment for bidding for public contract awards according to Community procurement rules; movement of workers (improvements for those legally established and their families). All these are reciprocal, but concessions are to be implemented in an 'asymmetric' way, meaning that the EC concessions are implemented first. The CEECs are also committed to introducing similar legislation to that applying in the Community concerning competition rules, including state aid; protection of intellectual, commercial, and industrial property; liberalization of payments and capital transfers in respect of trade and investments; and approximation of laws in other areas affecting the implementation of the Agreements. Implementation of all aspects of the Europe Agreements is a vast and far-reaching task.

The choice of the association formula for the Europe Agreements has had important political and legal repercussions. Article 238 stipulates that association agreements create reciprocal rights and obligations for the contracting parties, common actions and special procedures. But, at least initially, the Europe Agreements were not seen by the EU side as preaccession agreements. The preamble to the Europe Agreements only recognized accession as the wish of the associated country, not as an objective of the EU.[2]

This stance, however, changed at the European Council in Copenhagen in June 1993, which stated that 'the associated countries of central and eastern Europe that so desire shall become members of the Union. Accession will take place as soon as a country is able to assume the obligations of membership by satisfying the economic and political conditions.'[3]

Less than a year later in 1994 the first two applications for membership, from Hungary and Poland, were presented to the Council of Ministers in Brussels. The remainder of the applications ensued in the summer and winter of 1995, with Slovenia following in June 1996.

Table 1.1: Dates of Application for EU Membership

Hungary	31.3.94
Poland	5.4.94
Romania	22.6.95
Slovakia	27.6.95
Latvia	13.10.95
Estonia	24.11.95
Lithuania	8.12.95
Bulgaria	14.12.95
Czech Republic	17.1.96
Slovenia	10.6.96

At the European Council in Essen in December 1994 the path towards membership was further clarified with agreement on a preaccession strategy. The objective was

> to provide a route plan for the associated countries as they prepare for accession. The essential element of the strategy is their progressive preparation for integration into the Internal Market of the Union... This strategy will be supported by the implementation of policies to promote

---

2.   For an assessment of the Europe Agreements see Marc Maresceau (ed.), *Enlarging the European Union* (London: Longman, 1997); Mario Nuti, *EU-CEECs Integration: Policies and Markets at Work* (Milan: Franco Angeli, 1997).

3.   European Council (1993), Presidency Conclusions, Copenhagen June 1993, *Bulletin of the European Communities*, 6 (1993).

integration through the development of infra-structure, co-operation in the framework of the Trans-European Networks, the promotion of intra-regional co-operation, environmental co-operation, as well as the CFSP [Common Foreign and Security Policy], co-operation in the areas of justice and home affairs, and in culture, education and training. This integration will be supported by the Phare programme.[4]

The key objective of Essen was to intensify the technical preparations for membership. The Council proposed that the Commission should make a White Paper on the main requirements of the internal market and this was presented to the European Council in Cannes in June 1995 and became a major part of the CEECs' preparations for membership. The White Paper on the Internal Market not only provides a guide to its functioning but suggests a logical sequence in which the associated countries should go about bringing their legislation into line with that in the Union. Legislation, to be effective, must be properly implemented and enforced, and so the White Paper also provides guidance on the necessary regulatory and administrative structures:

> The principal responsibility for implementing the White Paper's recommendations lies with the associated countries themselves. The sooner their laws, conformity tests, standards institutes, and judicial procedures, are adapted to those in the Union, the sooner their businesses will feel the benefit. However, the Union recognizes that advice and support are needed and so the Commission established in 1996 a Technical Assistance Information Exchange Office (TAIEX) for the purpose which draws on the experience of the Member States in transposing Union legislation into national law in order to advise partners in central and eastern Europe. The Commission is now working with each associated country to devise its own strategy for alignment with the Internal Market, taking into account its economic situation and reform priorities.[5]

The Phare technical assistance programme is the EU's principal financial instrument for supporting the efforts of the applicants to prepare for membership. Between 1995 and 1999, the Phare budget is 6.7 billion ECU, and in the ten years from 1989 to 1999, Phare will have delivered a total of 11 billion ECU in assistance to the applicant countries—making it the largest technical assistance programme in history.

4.   European Council (1994), Presidency Conclusions, Essen, December 1994, *Bulletin of the European Communities*, 12 (1994).

5.   European Commission, White Paper on the Preparations of the Associated Countries of Central and Eastern Europe for Integration into the Internal Market of the Union, May 1995 (COM(95)163).

Phare includes a number of distinct programmes. The 'national' programmes are directed at a particular country; multicountry programmes address a specific issue in several countries; and cross-border programmes promote the cooperation among regions across borders. Each of these programmes can provide know-how transfer (advice, studies, technical assistance), supply of equipment, or investment cofinancing. Their implementation concerns practically all ministries and other public bodies as well civil society and business organizations. A large number of people are involved directly or indirectly.

Phare's flexibility has been increased through the adoption of multi-annual indicative programmes and increased focus on support for accession preparation by concentrating on infrastructure (75 per cent) and institution building (25 per cent). Applicant countries may also use up to 10 per cent of their national Phare allocations to fund their participation in Community programmes.

The structured dialogue consists of meetings of heads of state and government and more frequent ministerial meetings in policy areas ranging from foreign affairs and justice/home affairs to economic, transport, research and environmental issues. These meetings not only give the candidates a sense of belonging to the EU family but also provide a valuable insight into the workings of the EU machinery. Initially there was some CEEC criticism of the structured dialogue as being neither structured nor a dialogue. But the problems were resolved as the meetings were better prepared and the participants became engaged in a more open exchange of views and became better acquainted with each other and the Community style. Never before have applicant countries been invited to participate on a regular basis in joint meetings with the institutions of the Union so far in advance of accession.

Trade Flows

In terms of trade relations between the EU and the CEECs, a massive reorientation has taken place in trade flows since 1989, with the Union today accounting for 60 per cent of the associated countries' trade. This compares, moreover, with less than 5 per cent for trade with the United States, and less than 2 per cent for trade with Japan. The reasons for this reorientation include the break-up of the old Communist Council for Mutual Economic Assistance (CMEA), which provided for barter trade arrangements between members, and the desire of the population in the CEECs to buy Western consumer goods.

The rapid liberalization of trade between the CEECs and the EU has led to some problems which may intensify in future. These include EU allegations of dumping and CEEC criticism of the EU's reluctance to extend free trade to agricultural products. The CEECs have also experienced growing trade deficits with the EU and a consequent worsening of their balance of payments position.

Table 1.2: EU–CEEC Trade Flows

Foreign Trade of CEECs (in percentage terms)

	Exports to 1989	Exports to 1996	Imports from 1989	Imports from 1996
EU 15	20	65	32	68
Other CEECs	46	10	41	11
Russia/NIS	22	13	18	8
Japan	1	1	1	1
Others	11	11	8	12

Source: EBRD (European Bank for Reconstruction and Development)

There would be little point in the Union opening up its markets to the associated countries if barriers remain in trade among the associated countries themselves. For this reason the Union strongly supports the Central European Free Trade Area (CEFTA) and its extension to all associated countries. As trade barriers fall, foreign direct investment (FDI) should increase, with further gains to productivity and competitiveness.

The flow of FDI towards the CEECs has been somewhat disappointing compared to the far greater flows to Asia and other regions. This has perhaps reflected the problems regarding infrastructure, regulatory and taxation systems. Most FDI has been concentrated in Hungary, Poland and the Czech Republic, with Estonia benefiting from considerable investment from its neighbour, Finland.[6]

6.   See Saul Estrin, Kirsty Hughes and Sarah Todd, 'The Nature and Scope of FDI in Central and Eastern Europe' (Working Paper Number 3; London: RIIA, 1997).

Figure 1.1: Trends in FDI in the CEECs

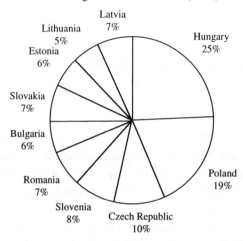

Percentage of FDI in CEECs (1995)

Immediately following the end of the Cold War there were high expectations in the CEECs that they would be welcomed into the Western institutions, notably the EU. It was a shock to recognize that their desire for early membership was not universally shared by EU Member States. The Europe Agreements contained no promise of membership but they were an essential component of the deepening relations between the CEECs and the Union. Gradually a fully fledged preaccession strategy was put into place involving technical and financial assistance, and a regular dialogue on a wide range of policy issues. As with the European Economic Area with the EFTA states, this was never going to be sufficient to satisfy the CEECs and hence it was only a matter of time before they applied for full membership of the EU.

2 |

The Process of Enlargement

This chapter explains the basic methods and procedures by which the European Union undertakes its enlargement. It draws on the experience of past enlargements, and anticipates progress in the present round, which effectively commenced with the European Council's conclusions in Copenhagen in June 1993, continues with the opening of negotiations with countries of Central and Eastern Europe in 1998, and is expected to lead to the accession of new members in the years following 2000.

The European Union has already behind it the experience of no fewer than 11 successfully concluded accession negotiations, which have led to nine accessions (on two occasions, with Norway, the conclusion of negotiations was followed by the negative results of referenda, which halted the process). The nine accessions have taken place in four successive waves of enlargement. The original six members were joined by the United Kingdom, Denmark and Ireland in a first wave in 1973. Then came Greece in 1981, and Spain and Portugal in 1986; this 'Iberian' enlargement is sometimes included with Greece as part of a 'southern' or 'Mediterranean' wave. Most recently in 1995 came Austria, Sweden and Finland, in an 'EFTA' enlargement.

This last was in fact the first enlargement of the European Union, the entity which came into being in November 1993 as a result of the Maastricht Treaty. Maastricht added two fields of cooperation (foreign and security policy, and justice and home affairs) to the already existing European Community (EC), itself a successor to the three original Communities (European Coal and Steel Community of 1951, European Economic Community and European Atomic Energy Community of 1957). For simplicity, the expression 'Union' rather than 'Community' is used in this chapter, even where the latter would be technically more correct.

The basic legal provision for extending the membership is to be found in Article O of the Union Treaty:

> Any European State may apply to become a Member of the Union. It shall address its application to the Council, which shall act unanimously after consulting the Commission and after receiving the assent of the European Parliament, which shall act by an absolute majority of its component members. The conditions of admission and the adjustments to the Treaties on which the Union is founded which such admission entails shall be the subject of an agreement between the Member States and the applicant State. This agreement shall be submitted for ratification by all the contracting States in accordance with their respective constitutional requirements.

This text has remained unchanged since Article 237 of the original EEC Treaty, except for the reference to the assent of the European Parliament which was added by the Single European Act in 1986. The coming into force of the Amsterdam Treaty will bring a further modification, for it will change the first sentence of Article O to read: 'Any European State which respects the principles in Article F (1) may apply to become a member of the Union'.

This introduces respect of the principles on which the Union is founded as one of the conditions, not just of membership, but even of application for membership; Article F (1) says 'the Union is founded on the principles of liberty, democracy, respect for human rights and fundamental freedoms, and the rule of law'.

It has often been remarked that Article O is an imperfect guide to enlargement. In the first place, it includes no geographical definition of Europe; perhaps wisely, the Union has never tried, in the treaties or elsewhere, to define officially the geographical limits of the Union. Nor does it include the political and economic conditions for membership, decided by the European Council at Copenhagen in 1993; originally, these conditions were designed for the countries of Central and Eastern Europe, but they are now accepted to be of general application. Moreover, Article O does not articulate clearly the different stages of the enlargement process which have developed in practice over the years (cf. Table 2.1) and which have become a well-established tradition.

Table 2.1: EU Membership—From Application to Accession

1. A European country submits an application for membership to the Council of the European Union.
2. The Council asks the Commission to deliver an Opinion on the application.
3. The Commission delivers its Opinion on the application to the Council.
4. The Council decides (unanimously) to open negotiations for accession.
5. Negotiations are opened between the Member States on the one hand, and each applicant individually on the other hand.
6. The Commission proposes, and the Council adopts (unanimously), positions to be taken by the Union vis-à-vis the applicants in accession negotiations.
7. Agreement reached between Union and applicant on a Draft Treaty of Accession.
8. Accession Treaty submitted to the Council and the European Parliament.
9. The Commission delivers another Opinion, on the Accession Treaty.
10. European Parliament delivers its assent to the Accession Treaty (by an absolute majority).
11. The Council approves the Accession Treaty (unanimously).
12. Member States and applicants formally sign the Accession Treaty.
13. Member States and applicants ratify the Accession Treaty.
14. After ratification, the Treaty comes into effect on the day of accession: the applicants become Member States.

As can be seen from Tables 2.2 and 2.3 the process of enlargement can be a lengthy and complicated affair. Previous enlargements of the Union have sometimes taken many years—in the case of the United Kingdom, Denmark and Ireland more than 11 years, if one counts from their first applications in 1961, and more than eight years in the case of Spain. The last enlargement was more rapidly conducted, taking less than three years for Finland.

The basic stages of the process—the application for membership, the Opinion, the opening of negotiations, the conclusion of negotiations, accession—merit a commentary.

The application for membership is an autonomous decision for the country concerned, and the Union has not officially encouraged or discouraged applications. Its attitude has been one of prudence, rather than of actively seeking to enlarge its membership, since there are normally sufficient problems to handle among existing members, without adding new ones. The historic decision of Copenhagen in July 1993, which promised membership to those of the associated countries in Central and Eastern Europe that so desired, was all the more exceptional since none of the countries had yet submitted an application. Within the next two years, all did so.

Table 2.2: Basic Stages of Enlargement

	A Application	B Opinion of Commission	C Opening of negotiations	D End of accession negotiations	E Date of accession
United Kingdom	10.5.67	29.9.67	30.6.70	22.1.72	1.1.73
Denmark	11.5.67	29.9.67	30.6.70	22.1.72	1.1.73
Ireland	11.5.67	29.9.67	30.6.70	22.1.72	1.1.73
Norway	21.7.67	29.9.67	30.6.70	22.1.72	(1.1.73)
Greece	12.6.75	29.1.76	27.7.76	28.5.79	1.1.81
Portugal	28.3.77	19.5.78	17.10.78	12.6.85	1.1.86
Spain	28.7.77	29.11.78	5.2.79	12.6.85	1.1.86
Turkey	14.4.87	14.12.89			
Austria	17.7.89	1.8.91	1.2.93	12.4.94	1.1.95
Cyprus	4.7.90	30.6.93			
Malta	16.7.90	30.6.93			
Sweden	1.7.91	31.7.92	1.2.93	12.4.94	1.1.95
Finland	18.3.92	4.11.92	1.2.93	12.4.94	1.1.95
Switzerland	26.5.92				
Norway	25.11.92	24.3.93	5.4.93	12.4.94	(1.1.95)

Notes:

Column A: Account is not taken in this table of the first round of applications of Ireland (31.7.61), United Kingdom (9.8.61), Denmark (10.8.61) and Norway (30.4.62); it led to the opening of negotiations with the United Kingdom (8.11.61) and subsequently with the others, but then to their suspension with the United Kingdom (29.1.63) and subsequently with the others.

Column D: 'End of negotiations' is date of signature of treaty, except for Austria, Sweden, Finland and Norway for which it is date of last session of accession conference.

Column E: Norway did not accede in 1973 or 1995 because of the 'no' in its referenda.

Table 2.3: Length of Stages of Enlargement

	Preparation of Opinion (A–B) months	Decision to open negotiations (B–C) months	Duration of negotiations (C–D) months	Total period (A–E) years/months
United Kingdom	5	33	19	5/7
Denmark	5	33	19	5/7
Ireland	5	33	19	5/7
Norway	2	33	19	(5/5)
Greece	7	6	34	5/6
Portugal	14	5	80	8/9
Spain	16	2	76	8/5
Turkey	32			
Austria	24	18	13	5/5
Cyprus	36			
Malta	35			
Sweden	13	6	13	3/6
Finland	8	3	13	2/9
Norway	4	1	12	(2/1)

Note: Periods are calculated to the nearest month.

It is clear from Tables 2.2 and 2.3 that the date of application bears no direct relationship to the date of accession. There is no advantage in making a 'premature' application—on the contrary, it can lead to a long period of waiting which may politically be negative rather than positive for the applicant country. But the timing of an application is naturally related to the applicant's view on when best to join the queue. Seniority in the queue gives a certain diplomatic precedence; for the negotiations with Austria, Sweden, Finland and Norway, the order of meetings was determined by the chronology of applications, so that Austria was normally received first. But this was not an invariable rule; it was not always an advantage for Austria; and the Treaty of Accession which resulted from the negotiations obeyed the rule of alphabetical order of the name of the country in its own language, which gave Norway (Norge), Austria (Österreich), Finland (Suomi), Sweden (Sverige).

The decision to apply for membership is a momentous decision for the country concerned, and triggers on the Union side the process described in Article O of the Treaty. The next important stage traditionally is the Commission's Opinion. Normally, the Council of Ministers requests the Opinion quite soon after the application for membership, but the time taken by the Commission to complete its Opinion has varied considerably. To some extent, this period is a function of the complexity of the economic and political questions to be analysed in the Opinion; but it is also a function of the rapidity with which the Union wants to proceed with the application, since until the Commission gives its Opinion, it is not customary to move to the stage of opening negotiations. Therefore, a delay of the Opinion can be seen as a pretext for postponing the opening of negotiations.

The Commission's Opinion is not a legal prerequisite of opening accession negotiations; Article O of the Treaty simply says that the Council 'shall act...after consulting the Commission', without determining the chronology of this consultation in relation to the accession negotiations. The Opinion of the Commission which precedes the negotiations is traditionally a lengthy analysis of the situation of the applicant country and the problems of membership—often prefiguring the list of subjects to be handled in the accession negotiations—and is designed to assist the Council in its decision on opening negotiations. At a later stage, there is another brief Opinion, delivered by the Commission after the completion of the negotiations.

Probably the most significant of the different stages of the accession process is the decision by the Union to open accession negotiations, not only because such negotiations require a large input of political and human resources, but also because opening them implies a willingness to conclude them. The commencement of accession negotiations creates new situations and new expectations, as both sides begin to take accession seriously and examine all its practical consequences.

The timing of the decision to conclude the negotiations depends at least as much on the applicant countries as on the Union, and for them it is related to factors such as the terms being offered by the Union, the progress of other applicants, and the domestic political situation. By the time that the decision to conclude negotiations has to be faced, a target date for accession is politically in the air and the constraints of the ratification timetable have begun to impose a discipline.

The final period, between the conclusion of negotiations and accession, is determined by the time necessary for ratification; with the increasing number of Member States, and the fact that the assent of the European Parliament is now required, the requirements of ratification are more onerous, and a year would seem to be the minimum time required to complete the procedures.

In the past, accessions have always taken place on 1 January of the year following the effective conclusion of negotiations. The choice of 1 January for the date of accession is based on practical considerations: it fits the Union's budgetary year and also the cycle of its institutions, particularly the six-monthly rotation of the presidency of the Council. To upset these internal balances by having an accession on, say, 1 July or 1 September, would create too many complications.

The Conduct of Negotiations

The procedure for accession negotiations, and the roles of the different participants, require particular comment, because an accession negotiation is not a typical external negotiation, in which the Commission is the spokesman on matters of Community competence. It is a kind of intergovernmental conference between the Member States and the applicant country. The Union's 'common positions', decided by the Council by unanimity, are normally presented to the applicant country by the presidency of the Council. The Commission, however, has an important role in proposing common positions to the Council, and it may be mandated by the Council to seek solutions with the applicant country.

The procedure for the conduct of negotiations is traditionally defined by a decision of the Council before negotiations commence. The text of this procedural decision has hardly been altered since it was first formulated in 1970, although there have been minor changes to take account of the Maastricht and Amsterdam Treaties. In 1997 the Council approved the following text, for the negotiations to begin in 1998:

1. The accession negotiations will be conducted by the European Union according to a uniform procedure at all levels and in relation to all problems.
2. Accordingly, the Council will determine the common position of the European Union on all problems posed by the accession negotiations.
3. In order to determine the common positions of the European Union, the Commission is invited to make proposals on all the problems posed by the accession negotiations in those areas which relate to the Treaties establishing the European Communities.

    Concerning matters related to CFSP and cooperation in the field of justice and home affairs, proposals will be made by the

Presidency, as a general rule, in close liaison with Member States and the Commission. It is also open to Member States to make proposals, and to the Commission to make proposals in the areas covered by Article J and Article K.1(1) to (6) of the Treaty on European Union.

4. In accordance with Article 151 of the EC Treaty, Coreper will have overall responsibility for preparing the deliberations of the Council concerning the establishment of the common positions.

    The Political Committee and the Coordinating Committee referred to in Article K.4 will act as consultation and coordination bodies, contributing to the definition of the common positions for matters relating to CFSP and to cooperation in the field of justice and home affairs respectively, the results of their work being submitted to Coreper.

5. On the European Union side, the negotiating meetings between the European Union and the applicants will be chaired at all levels by the Presidency-in-Office of the Council.

6. The common position of the European Union will be set out and upheld in the negotiations with the applicant countries either by the President of the Council or, where the Council so decides, by the Commission, particularly if existing Community policies are concerned.

7. When the negotiations are conducted at the level of Permanent Representatives and in the working parties that will be established, the rules set out in paragraphs 5 and 6 above will apply.

8. In addition, the Council declares itself ready to give the Commission the task of seeking possible solutions, in contact with the applicant countries, to certain problems arising in the course of negotiations and reporting to the Council, which will give it the necessary guidance for the subsequent continuation of this task in order to identify points of agreement to be submitted to the Council.

    This arrangement will apply in particular when existing common policies are concerned (*Agence Europe*, 9 December 1997).

The Council's decision on internal procedures is complemented by a further procedural decision, agreed with the applicant country, on the organization of the Accession Conference. Traditionally it determines, among other things, that:

- sessions are held either at the level of ministers or at the level of deputies (that is, ambassadors; in the case of the Member States, their permanent representatives in Brussels);
- the secretariat of the Conference comprises members of the Council's Secretariat, and persons designated by the applicant country;

- the costs of the Conference (rent, equipment, telecommunications, interpretation, and so on) are defrayed jointly by the participants.

Finally a decision is taken on the list of chapters for negotiation; for the negotiations in 1998, a list of 31 chapters was drawn up (cf. Table 2.4).

Table 2.4: Provisional Indicative List of Chapter Headings

1. Free movement of goods
2. Freedom of movement for persons
3. Freedom to provide services
4. Free movement of capital
5. Company law
6. Competition policy
7. Agriculture
8. Fisheries
9. Transport policy
10. Taxation
11. Economic and monetary union
12. Statistics
13. Social policy and employment
14. Energy
15. Industrial policy
16. Small and medium-sized undertakings
17. Science and research
18. Education and training
19. Telecommunications and information technologies
20. Culture and audiovisual policy
21. Regional policy and coordination of structural instruments
22. Environment
23. Consumers and health protection
24. Cooperation in the fields of justice and home affairs
25. Customs union
26. External relations
27. Common Foreign and Security Policy
28. Financial control
29. Financial and budgetary provisions
30. Institutions
31. Other

(Note: This list in no way prejudices the decisions to be taken at an appropriate stage in the negotiations or the order in which the subjects will be dealt with.)

The object of an accession negotiation—admission to the Union—already distinguishes it from other types of negotiations: it is not aimed at an agreement between the Union on the one hand and an external partner on the other, as is the normal case in international negotiations, but with the way in which an applicant country will function as a member. It is concerned with how the 'external' becomes 'internal'.

Representatives of the Union's institutions—particularly the Commission and the General Secretariat of the Council—are in the first place agents of the Union and its existing members, but also have a wider responsibility towards the applicant countries as future members. The Council Secretariat has the role of secretariat of the Accession Conference. The Commission's role is less prominent than in a normal international negotiation, in which it is the spokesman on questions of 'Community competence'; in an accession negotiation, the spokesman is normally the presidency, and the Commission has a secondary role. But this is more a matter of form than of fact: the Commission has traditionally been an important interlocutor of applicant countries, and this privileged relationship functions well if representatives of the Commission take account in advance of their responsibility to the enlarged Union—that is, when they treat applicant countries as future members. It has been said that the Commission's role vis-à-vis the applicant country is to be the 'friend who tells the truth', an observation that reflects the fact that an applicant country—particularly in the early stages of its application and negotiations—tends to receive excessively positive and optimistic reactions from its contacts with individual Member States.

The role of the Commission in accession negotiations is principally to make proposals to the Council for 'common positions' of the Union; it may also be entrusted by the Council with the task of seeking solutions with the applicants. Naturally it bases its proposals for common positions on exploratory talks, and on an informal judgment of what the applicant country may in the end be prepared to accept, tempered with a judgment of how far the Member States would be prepared to go.

It is not an exaggeration to say that the most lengthy and arduous part of the negotiations is not the Accession Conference between the Union and the applicant countries at ministerial or ambassadorial level, but the internal discussions of the Union itself. The sessions of the Accession Conference in 1993–1994 were rather formal, with each side reading prepared statements, except in the very last days of the negotiations. It was among the 12, in the Committee of Permanent Representatives

(Coreper), or in the Council's Enlargement Group which reported to Coreper, that the longest debates took place.

The difficulty of reaching agreement on the Union side is a function, naturally, of the fact that all decisions on common positions have to be reached by unanimity, not qualified majority. This factor tends to prolong discussion and render the task of Commission and Presidency difficult, since it is necessary to satisfy all Member States. From the point of view of the applicants, it is desirable not only to have 'friends' among the Member States, but also to have no 'enemies' strongly opposed to their requests.

The Importance of the *'acquis'*

An important aspect of accession negotiations has always been the insistence of the existing Member States that the applicant country should accept the 'acquis'—that is, the body of laws and rules which have been developed over the years—without significant change. The precise formulation used by the Union in the last enlargement is worth quoting, in the words used by the President of Council (the Danish Foreign Minister) at the opening of negotiations on 1 February 1993:

> Accession implies full acceptance by your countries of the actual and potential rights and obligations attaching to the Community system and its institutional framework, known as the *'acquis communautaire'*. This includes:
> * the content, principles and political objectives of the Treaties, including those of the Maastricht Treaty;
> * legislation adopted pursuant to the Treaties, and the case law of the Court of Justice;
> * statements and resolutions adopted within the Community framework;
> * international Agreements and Agreements concluded among themselves by the Member States relating to Community activities.
> The acceptance of these rights and obligations by a new member may give rise to technical adjustments, and exceptionally to temporary (not permanent) derogations and transitional arrangements to be defined during the accession negotiations, but can in no way involve amendments to Community rules.

A similar formulation applies for the present round of enlargement, with the notion of *'acquis communautaire'* now being subsumed into the broader notion of *'acquis* of the Union', and the Amsterdam Treaty now also forming part of the *acquis*.

One may justifiably ask, in light of such a position, what there is left for an applicant country to negotiate with the Union, if none of the rules can be changed and only technical adjustments and temporary derogations are possible. Why does the Union take such a hard line?

Traditionally, international agreements between two parties are based on the concept of a mutually balanced agreement, involving concessions and counter-concessions, and advantages for both sides. Accession negotiations are less symmetrical. From the point of view of the Union it is the applicant who has requested to join, not vice versa; and it has done so because it believes that membership offers advantages. Among those advantages, not least is the right to participate and vote in the Union's institutions from the very first day of membership; that is why the statement quoted emphasized the 'rights' equally with the 'obligations' of membership. From the point of view of the applicant, the priority must be to join the Union, rather than to seek basic changes in its rules—it being understood that, as a member, it will be in a position to pursue it own interests, like other members. It has even been remarked that accession negotiations are essentially concerned with 'obtaining a microphone and a name-plate': that is, a seat and voice in the Council of Ministers and the other institutions, on equal terms with the existing members.

Nor should it be forgotten that, in granting concessions to an applicant country in respect of a given rule, the Union can easily find itself reopening old discussions and old compromises which were necessary for the adoption of the rule. Naturally the Member States tend to regard the applicant's request for special treatment through the prism of their own national interests, taking account of concessions given or taken in the past, and potential concessions in the future. In this sense, the representatives of applicant countries can be forgiven for thinking occasionally that the negotiation between them and the Union is an intrusion by them into an ongoing negotiation among the existing Member States. Against this background, the emphasis on the *'acquis'* in accession negotiations should also be understood as a way by which the Union minimizes the risk of reopening hard-won decisions and compromises.

3 |

The Preparation of the Opinions

Early in 1996, the Commission began collecting the necessary information for the preparation of its Opinions on the ten countries of Central and Eastern Europe. Opinions had already been made on Cyprus
and Malta in 1993 and on Turkey in 1989. The main object of the
Opinions was the traditional one: an assessment of the candidates' capacity to assume the obligations of membership. In addition, the Commission had to take into account the political and economic conditions
defined by the European Council in Copenhagen in June 1993, which
stated that membership of the Union requires

> that the candidate has achieved stability of institutions guaranteeing
> democracy, the rule of law, human rights and respect for and protection
> of minorities; the existence of a functioning market economy, as well as
> the capacity to cope with competitive pressure and market forces within
> the Union; the ability to take on the obligations of membership, includ-
> ing adherence to the aims of political, economic and monetary union.[1]

The Copenhagen European Council added a further criterion, linking
enlargement to institutional reform, when it concluded that 'the Union's
capacity to absorb new members, while maintaining the momentum of
European integration, is also an important consideration in the general
interest of both the Union and the candidate countries'. However, this
'fourth criterion', which concerns the development of the Union, was
not the object of the Opinions, which focused on the situation of the
candidates.

The Madrid European Council in December 1995 referred also to the
need to create the conditions for the gradual, harmonious integration of
the candidate countries particularly through:

- the development of the market economy
- the adjustment of their administrative structures
- the creation of a stable economic and monetary environment.

1.   Conclusions of the European Council, Copenhagen, June 1993.

The European Council in Madrid also gave a new impetus to the enlargement process by asking the Commission:

- to take its evaluation of the effects of enlargement on Community policies further, particularly with regard to agricultural and structural policies;
- to expedite preparation of its Opinions, so that they can be forwarded to the Council as soon as possible after the conclusion of the Inter-governmental Conference;
- to embark upon preparation of 'a composite paper on enlargement', to complement the Opinions by providing an overall approach;
- to submit a communication on the future financial framework of the Union, having regard to the prospect of enlargement, immediately after the conclusion of the Intergovernmental Conference [IGC].[2]

This implied that the Commission had to forward to the Council a comprehensive package of communications on enlargement after the conclusion of the IGC which commenced in March 1996.

In its Opinions on the applications for membership, the Commission had to make an assessment of the situation of each applicant country together with an evaluation of its capacity to take on the obligations of membership. In approaching this task, the Commission was confronted with a number of problems which rendered the exercise more difficult than for previous Opinions. In the first place, it had never before had to handle simultaneously as many as ten Opinions on applications for membership; the Opinions on Greece, Portugal, Spain, Turkey, Austria, Sweden, Finland and Norway had all been issued separately; only in the case of Malta and Cyprus had there been a simultaneous finalization of Opinions. In fact, there had been a single 'combined' Opinion on the UK, Denmark, Norway and Ireland in 1967, and the possibility of doing the same for the ten Central and Eastern European countries was considered. But it was soon decided to proceed with ten separate documents, to emphasize the fact that the applications were considered on their individual merits rather than as a group; the Opinions on each country would be self-contained, without comparisons with other candidates or references to other Opinions. This approach rendered it all the more necessary to include an overall document, bringing together the main conclusions and 'horizontal' questions raised by the Opinions.

A second problem was the absence of detailed information on important aspects of the candidate countries. The majority of them had only

2. Conclusions of the European Council, Madrid, December 1995.

just been created, or recreated: the three Baltic states had regained their independence, Slovenia had separated from Yugoslavia, and the Czech and Slovak Republics had been created from the divorce of Czechoslovakia. There were consequently basic problems of statistics, and comparability of statistics. There was also an absence of information about the legislative situation, which in any case was changing rapidly in these countries as they consolidated their new states and made their political and economic transition. Because of the administrative changes and reforms which they were undergoing, and the lack of suitably experienced staff in ministries, it was difficult even for the countries themselves to formulate a clear analysis of their situation in relation to the EU.

Thirdly, the gap between these countries and the existing Member States in terms of economic and social development is greater than in the case of any previous enlargement. Their average level of income, measured in GDP per head (compared by means of 'purchasing power standards') is only about a third of that of the average of the Union, although this average conceals a wide range of variation, with Slovenia and the Czech Republic at rather more than a half of the Union's average, and the three Baltic states, Bulgaria and Romania at around a quarter. Although the level of economic development does not figure among the criteria for membership defined at Copenhagen, there is manifestly a certain correlation between it and the level of administrative capacity and ability to operate the quite complex legal and regulatory systems required by a modern market economy. The existence of this wide economic and social gap, and the number of areas where progress was needed to conform with the requirements of EU membership, made it clear that the Opinions would have to contain a detailed analysis.

Finally, it was clear from the outset that the political significance of the exercise would be all the more important because of the number of competing applicant countries. Although the Copenhagen European Council had given the promise that all ten countries would become members of the Union, the decision to be taken in the light of the Opinions was nevertheless a very important one, namely whether or not to open negotiations for membership. In what order of ranking would the Commission place the countries as a result of its assessment? Would it differentiate between them in its recommendations, or would it recommend to open negotiations with all? This dimension of the exercise made it necessary to ensure scrupulous equality of treatment in the analysis, and a secure basis of comparison for the conclusions.

Within the Commission in early 1996, the necessary organization was developed with the setting up of an 'interservice group' to coordinate the contributions of each 'service' or Directorate General to the exercise, and the creation of a small 'Enlargement Team' in Directorate General IA which was responsible for relations with the Central and Eastern European countries. The first task was to ensure adequate sources of information. A certain amount of data was already available, through bilateral relations with the countries concerned, the association agreements, reports from the Commission's delegations in the countries, and international organizations. In addition, the decision was taken to request detailed information from the countries themselves by means of a 'questionnaire', as had been the case in the preparation of previous Opinions.

To establish the factual situation for its Opinions, the Commission therefore relied to a considerable extent on information provided by applicant countries. In April 1996 it sent to the ten countries a series of questions covering all the main areas of the *'acquis'* in the form of a questionnaire of 150 pages with 23 chapters, asking for economic, statistical and legislative information. The areas covered, beginning with customs and taxation, continuing with agriculture and fisheries, and concluding with foreign and security policy and justice and home affairs, corresponded essentially to the third criterion of Copenhagen, that is the capacity to take on the obligations of membership. The extract which follows illustrates the nature of the questions.

Extract from the Commission questionnaire sent to candidate countries on 26 April 1996

Customs

1. Have you evaluated the impact of the dismantling of the customs controls at the borders with EU Member States and future neighbouring acceding countries? Do you have any long-term strategy in this field?
2. Please specify the elements of your legislation that may be analogous to duties or charges having equivalent effect (Articles 9 to 17 of the Union Treaty) that should be abolished before accession.
3. Please provide a copy of your country's legislation regarding reliefs from customs duty, and treatment of counterfeit and pirated goods.

4. Does your country operate a system of tariff quotas on any imported goods (the application of a lower than normal rate of duty to a predetermined quantity of goods)?

5. Does your country operate a system of tariff suspensions (the application of a lower rate of duty, irrespective of the quantity of goods)?

6. Do you have a binding tariff information system? If so, are there any similarities with the system used in the EU? (Article 12 of Council Regulation [EEC] No 2913/92)

7. If any of the following economic customs procedures are not currently applied or actively supported in national law, how would it be envisaged to put these regimes into force at the time of accession? If they are currently applied, please describe precisely their conditions for operation:
    *   customs warehouses
    *   inward processing
    *   outward processing
    *   processing under customs control
    *   temporary importation.

8. How many free zones are currently operational? Where are they situated?

9. In the context of the controls on passenger's baggage in airports, do the airports which are likely to be designated as Community international airports (under Articles 190 (b) and 197 of Commission Regulation No. 2454/93) have an infrastructure which will enable the implementation of the measures provided for in Articles 190 to 197 of the said Regulation and, in particular, of Article 195?

10. Please describe your country's legislation for the prevention, the detection and the prosecution of operations contrary to the customs legislation.

The Commission was also faced with the problem of obtaining information relevant to the first and second criteria mentioned at Copenhagen, that is the 'political' conditions relating to democracy, rule of law, human rights, and minorities, and the 'economic' conditions relating to the existence of a market economy. It was decided not to pose a detailed series of questions on these matters, but simply to invite the applicant countries, in the introduction to the questionnaire, to make observations on the situation of their country, and particularly to give a summary of their constitutional and institutional framework, and their membership of international organizations.

Initially this questionnaire was greeted with suspicion and even distrust by the applicant countries. To reply to all these questions within three months required an enormous effort of organization and manpower; it was perceived as a new imposition, even a tactic for delay on the part of Brussels. Nevertheless, the questionnaire had an important impact in the applicant countries, encouraging them to understand more fully the extent and scope of EU policies, and to review their administrative arrangements for coordination of EU-integration affairs. The replies to the questionnaires were received from all the countries by the end of July 1996, and were verified by the Commission, taking into account information and analyses from many other sources.

If the compilation of the replies to the questionnaire was a difficult task for the applicant countries, the analysis of the voluminous replies was a serious test of the Commission's own organizational capacity. The ten sets of replies, estimated to contain 30,000 pages (without counting the annexes), arrived at the end of July, just when most officials in Brussels were preparing to leave for holiday in August. Nevertheless, they were rapidly sorted and distributed to the different services, many officials worked in August, and a first assessment was ready in September, leading to a series of supplementary questions to the applicant countries in the autumn.

In the following nine months, until the Opinions were finalized in July 1997, there was an intensive process of analysis, comparison, and dialogue within the Commission, with the applicant countries, and with others concerned. The Commission did not officially consult the Council, the Parliament, the Member States, or any other organization about the contents of the Opinions—they were, after all, to be the Commission's own Opinions and its own responsibility. Neither the analysis nor the conclusions of the Opinions were shown to anyone for comment, and the draft texts were kept a well-guarded secret until their final approval. But naturally the Commission took account of information and representations from many quarters. For the political criteria, it obtained useful information and assessments from the Member States, from the Council of Europe, and from the High Commissioner for Minorities of the Organization for Security and Cooperation in Europe (OSCE), as well as from non-governmental organizations and academic circles. For the economic criteria, the Commission's Directorate General for Economic Affairs drew on material from all the relevant international bodies such as the European Bank for Reconstruction and Development (EBRD), the World Bank, the Organization for Economic Cooperation and Development (OECD), as well as academic sources, and on its ongoing dialogue with the applicant countries and with the Member States.

Within the Commission, each of more than 20 different services made a comprehensive evaluation, for its field of responsibility, of the situation and prospects of each of the ten countries. Their inputs were analysed and condensed by the coordinators in DG 1A, conducting an iterative process in which questions and assessments were continuously refined. Those involved have confirmed that in this 'interservice' work the emphasis was on objective and independent analysis. Although it was evident that the politically crucial aspect of the exercise would be the relative evaluation or 'ranking' of the ten countries, no guidance was given by the coordinators in DG 1A to the other services on the expected or desired results of their analyses; and no instructions were given to the coordinators by their superiors at the political level in the Commission on the order in which the countries should be ranked for 'political' reasons. The exercise generated a genuinely independent set of analyses from the various arms of the Commission, on which the final assessment was based.

What methodology was developed for evaluating the Copenhagen criteria? In the first place, the Commission had to take a view on the time horizon involved. Given the gap still existing between even the better-prepared countries and the Union's requirements, it was obvious that if the Opinions had addressed the question 'Do these countries fulfil the conditions of membership at the present time?'—which was more or less the question addressed by Opinions in the past—the conclusion would have been 'no' for all of them. On the other hand, the analysis could hardly be conducted on the basis of the question 'Will these countries fulfil the conditions at some (unspecified) date in the future?' to which the conclusion would have to be 'yes'.

The Commission accordingly developed the notion of the 'medium-term' time horizon for the Opinions. In assessing each country in respect of the economic criteria and capacity to assume the *acquis*, it included in each Opinion a prospective assessment, attempting to evaluate the progress which could reasonably be expected on the part of each country in the years before accession. It stated that 'for this purpose, and without prejudging the actual date of accession, the Opinion is based on a medium-term time horizon of approximately five years'.

The services of the Commission, making their evaluations in the autumn of 1996 and the spring of 1997, were thus invited to look forward to the year 2002 as a hypothetical date for accession. Even this technical assumption provoked some initial criticism, since the year 2000 had been mentioned in speeches by leaders such as Chancellor Kohl and President Chirac as a point of reference for enlargement, and it was not for the Commission to enter into a public dispute with them. But as time passed, the year 2002 began to be accepted more widely as a realistic, even optimistic, time horizon, taking into account negotiations beginning in 1998, and lasting longer than with Austria, Sweden, and Finland (one year) but it was to be hoped less long than with Spain and Portugal (seven years). The conclusion of negotiations within three years followed by one year for ratification of a treaty appeared to be a reasonable basis for calculation, giving the year 2002 as a possible date for the first accessions.

For the evaluation of the political criteria, however, the Commission did not employ a time horizon, but based itself on the present-day situation, without attempting to assess what might happen in the future. This was partly because of the inherent difficulty of predicting the course of events relating to democracy, human rights and so on. But it was also because of a conviction that priority should be accorded to the political criteria, compared to the other criteria. While one could envisage opening negotiations for membership with a country whose administrative, legislative and economic conditions still required improvement, how could one open negotiations with a country not yet deemed to be democratic? The Commission's view, formed at an early stage of the exercise, that 'respect of the political conditions is a necessary, but not a sufficienct, condition for opening accession negotiations' was corroborated by the decision at the Amsterdam European Council in June 1997 to amend the Treaty's basic provision (Article O) in such a way as to make respect of democracy and human rights an explicit condition of applying for membership.

The time frame for completion of the Opinions had been defined as 'as soon as possible after the conclusion of the Intergovernmental Conference' which commenced in March 1996. In the early months of 1997 it became clear that there was a good chance, although not a certainty, that it would conclude at the European Council to be held in Amsterdam in June 1997. Consequently the Commission prepared itself for the adoption of the Opinions, and the other documents associated with Agenda 2000, in mid-July. The applicant countries were given the signal that if they wished to submit further information to the

Commission or update their replies to the questionnaire of 1996, they should do so by May. A round of 'pre-Opinion' visits to the applicant countries by the Commissioner responsible, Hans van den Broek, and by senior officials, was completed, but no indications were given to them as to the conclusions of the Opinions. No conclusions were in fact drawn up, even in a provisional form, until the very last stages of the exercise in late June.

The conclusion of the IGC at the Amsterdam European Council on 17 June opened the way for launching the next stage of the enlargement process. Political interest in the Opinions began to mount, particularly with the prospect of the NATO ministerial meeting in Madrid on 8 July which was to take key decisions on the enlargement of NATO. It invited only Poland, Hungary and the Czech Republic to become members, leaving other countries of Central and Eastern Europe disappointed: the hopes of the three Baltic states for positive signs were rebuffed, and Romania and Slovenia, which had made efforts of persuasion up to the last moment, had to content themselves with an honourable mention in the NATO conclusions. This decision for a limited expansion of NATO heightened interest in the Commission's conclusions: would it likewise take a limited view, perhaps recommending that negotiations be opened with just three countries of Central and Eastern Europe—the same three as NATO?

Another cause of speculation was one of the conclusions of the Intergovernmental Conference at Amsterdam. Although it failed to take concrete decisions on institutional reform of the EU in advance of enlargement, it agreed on a protocol with guidelines for limited reforms to come into force at the next enlargement, and provision for more fundamental reforms at another IGC in the following terms: 'at least one year before the membership of the EU exceeds twenty, a conference of representatives of the Governments of Member States shall be convened in order to carry out a comprehensive review of the provisions of the Treaties on the composition and functioning of the Institutions'. The basic reason why a membership of 20 was mentioned was that the reforms for the next enlargement included the limitation of the number of Commissioners to one per Member State; and since the present number of Commissioners is 20, such a reform can take place without an increase in the number of Commissioners, as long as there are no more than 20 Member States. However, this mention of enlargement to 20 members as a threshold beyond which another IGC would be necessary prompted the idea that the next enlargement would be limited to five, and the accession negotiations limited to the same number; and since the opening of negotiations had already been promised to Cyprus, there was room in the negotiations for only four (or, to be on the safe side, three) countries of Central and Eastern Europe.

Against this background, there were intensive discussions in the Commission, towards the end of June and in early July, which led to its decision to recommend the opening of negotiations with five countries of Central and Eastern Europe (Hungary, Poland, Estonia, the Czech Republic, Slovenia) at the same time as with Cyprus. In political terms, it was a courageous decision to differentiate between the ten applicant countries on the basis of their degree of readiness for membership. In geopolitical terms, it made good sense to encompass a larger number of countries than the three countries chosen for NATO, and to include not only three geographically central countries (Poland, the Czech Republic and Hungary) but also a country to the north (Estonia) and one in the south (Slovenia). The next chapter gives in more detail the objective analyses which led to these conclusions.

4 |

The Contents of the Opinions

Before providing a summary of each of the Commission's Opinions, this chapter gives a commentary on their general structure and contents. For reasons of space, it is not possible to include extensive passages from the full Opinions, which run to more than a hundred pages each. It should be borne in mind that the summaries are highly selective and condensed versions of longer texts, and give only the essential arguments and conclusions.

General Structure and Contents

The structure of the ten Opinions is identical—and this reflects the wish of the Commission to show that all ten countries were evaluated according to the same methods and criteria. A brief preface recalls the application for membership, and the general political context, and is followed by an account of relations between the applicant country and the Union. This account includes a rapid historical survey, placing each country in the broad sweep of European history, and then recounting in more detail developments since 1989–90, including the Europe Agreement, and the country's official statements on its approach to membership of the Union. There follows a brief description of the preaccession strategy, including phare, the White Paper on the Internal Market, the structured dialogue, participation in Community programmes, bilateral trade relations and finally an evaluation of the functioning of the Europe Agreement.

The evaluation of the functioning of the Europe Agreement is essentially positive for all the countries, although a critical note is struck in some cases with mention of bilateral disputes. The catalogue of problems concerning Poland is quite long:

> there have been a number of implementation difficulties in the trade field, notably regarding the Polish import surcharge, certification, steel

industry restructuring, motor vehicle sector measures, measures in the oil sector and export restrictions on hides and skins. The number of bilateral trade problems has tended to overshadow the general perception of the bilateral relationship. But most of these problems have been resolved.

With the Czech Republic 'there have been few trade problems, though recently important trade-related problems have arisen (notably the import deposit scheme). There is room for enhanced dialogue and co-operation to prevent such issues from developing. The Czech Republic has at times shown signs of reluctance to acknowledge difficulties and seek a collaborative approach to resolving them'. The main body of the Opinions is divided into four parts, as can be seen from the summaries that follow later in this chapter.

1. *Political Criteria*
This section of the Opinions describes and evaluates each country in respect of the different 'political' elements mentioned in the Copenhagen criteria. Covered under 'democracy and the rule of law' are parliament and the legislature (with an evaluation of its functioning, including the results of the most recent elections), the executive structure (including the respective roles of president and prime minister, local government, laws governing the public administration, and civilian control of army secret services and police) and the judiciary (with comments on its degree of independence, the roles of supreme court and constitutional court, and the offices of public prosecutor, ombudsman and so on).

A thread running through all the Opinions is the critical reference to the problems facing the judicial system because of the inadequate number, training and status of judges, and the resulting inefficiency in terms of the time taken to hand down judgments. Other specific criticisms are made in some cases (for example, lack of independence of radio and television) and in particular in the case of Slovakia, there are a number of criticisms of the treatment of the opposition in parliament, the lack of respect of the government for other institutions (the President of the Republic, the constitutional court and so on) and the independence of the judiciary.

Under 'human rights and the protection of minorities' are, first, an evaluation of civil and political rights, including the situation concerning the death penalty, freedom of association and expression (written press and audiovisual), rights to property, refugees, nationality questions, freedom to belong to trade unions, and freedom of education and religion; and, secondly, an important section on minority rights, which describes the numbers of existing minorities, their status under the law, and treatment by the public authorities.

In most of the countries, the problems of the Roma (gypsy) community are highlighted; although their situation is different from that of 'national' minorities, they are frequently victims of social exclusion. The situation of the various national minorities is also analysed, and in the case of Slovakia there are critical remarks on the absence of a language law for the Hungarian minority. There are important passages on the mainly Russian-speaking minorities in Estonia and Latvia: in terms of numbers, the minorities in these two Baltic states are by far the most significant ones in the applicant countries (non-citizens constitute 28 per cent of the population in Latvia and 25 per cent in Estonia) and in both cases the Opinions recommend that measures be taken to accelerate naturalization procedures, and ensure equality of treatment for minorities.

Although these reservations figure clearly in the 'general evaluation' for Estonia and Latvia, and there is a discreet qualification also for Bulgaria and Romania (which are only 'on the way' to satisfying the political criteria), it is only for Slovakia that the Commission's evaluation of the political criteria is overall negative.

2. *Economic Criteria*

This section begins with a survey of the economic situation, describing the progress of each country in key areas of economic transformation: liberalization of the price and trade system, stabilization of the economy, structural change, and reform of the financial sector. It includes indicators of economic structure and the main economic trends in recent years (1994, 1995, 1996), together with comments on the situation of external trade, foreign exchange, and social and regional indicators.

It then assesses the economy in the perspective of membership, analysing in turn the two elements mentioned in the Copenhagen criteria: the existence of a functioning market economy, and the capacity to cope with competitive pressure and market forces within the Union. On the first element, the analysis in the Opinions reflects the generally accepted views of economists on the process of economic transition:

> The existence of a market economy requires equilibrium between supply and demand to be established by the free interplay of market forces. A market economy is functioning when the legal system, including the regulation of property rights, is in place and can be enforced. The performance of a market economy is facilitated and improved by macroeconomic stability and a degree of consensus about the essentials of economic policy. A well-developed financial sector and an absence of significant barriers to market entry and exit help improve the efficiency with which an economy works.

On the second element, the Opinions frankly admit that 'it is difficult, some years ahead of prospective membership, and before the applicant country has adopted and implemented the larger part of Community law, to form a definitive judgement of the country's ability to fulfil this criterion.' Nevertheless a number of pertinent features are identified and assessed, including the stabilization of the macroeconomic environment, the quality of human and physical capital including education, training and infrastructure, the degree of economic integration already achieved with the Union, the structure of ownership and production (benefits from the single market may be greater in sectors where there is a higher proportion of small firms, which are more affected by trade barriers), the quantity and quality of investment, and the legal system and the banking sector.

After reviewing prospects and priorities, and commenting on the economic strategy for the medium term, this section concludes with a 'general evaluation' of the extent to which the applicant country meets the two economic criteria. The Commission finds that five countries (Czech Republic, Estonia, Hungary, Poland, Slovenia) can already be considered as functioning market economies, even if important aspects still need to be developed, and a sixth (Slovakia) comes near to satisfying this criterion. On the capacity to withstand competitive pressure, the Commission finds that two countries (Hungary and Poland) should satisfy this criterion in the medium term if they stay on their present course, three countries (Czech Republic, Slovakia, Slovenia) should do so if they strengthen their efforts, and another country (Estonia) comes close to them, having modernized and radically liberalized its economy.

3. *Ability to Assume the Obligations of Membership*
This section of the Opinions examines all the sectors and policies concerned by the adoption of the *acquis*, beginning with the internal market, continuing with economic affairs, sectoral policies (agriculture,

transport and so on), regional policy, environmental policy and external policies (trade, foreign and security policy) and concluding with financial control and the budgetary implications of membership.

For each of these fields, the Opinions give a brief commentary on the nature of the *acquis* (including mention of the Europe Agreement and the White Paper, where relevant) and a descriptive summary providing a kind of 'photograph' of the economic and legislative situation in the country. This is followed by a 'current and prospective assessment' which evaluates progress achieved so far, and mentions the deficiencies which need to be remedied for the country to implement fully the *acquis*. There is then a 'conclusion' which gives a brief reply to the question 'Can this country be expected to take on satisfactorily the obligations of membership in the medium term?'

Naturally, the reply to this question is often qualified, even if the reply is basically positive. To take just two examples, the conclusion for Hungary in the chapter on financial control is 'in the medium term, Hungary should be able to fulfil its obligations in relation to financial control without any major problems, provided that measures currently envisaged are put into place'; and for Slovenia in the chapter on agriculture (after reference to particular efforts needed in different areas for strengthening, enforcing, and restructuring) the conclusion is: 'if such progress is accomplished, accession in the medium term should not be accompanied by significant problems in applying the common agricultural policy in an appropriate manner'. Only in a minority of cases is there a categorical 'yes', such as the conclusion for the Czech Republic in the chapter on fisheries: 'this sector should not represent a problem for accession' (which is hardly surprising, since the country has no coastline, and inland fisheries are limited to a few thousand tons).

A diligent effort to compare the precise formulation of these sectoral conclusions in the ten Opinions reveals in most cases a differentiation between the candidates; it is not difficult to decipher the codes which the Commission's experts have used to signify their relative evaluation of the ten countries for each part of the *acquis*.

What is more difficult is to define an overall 'ranking order' of the ten countries in the section of the Opinions concerning their capacity to take on the obligations of membership; the Commission makes no overall summary and evaluation in this section, as it does in others, and leaves its general conclusions to the end of the Opinion. This is hardly surprising, since such an evaluation would require at least an implicit weighting of the relative importance of each of the different parts of the *acquis*, an enterprise with all kinds of problems, both technical and political, and unlikely to lead to agreed results within the Community institutions. Two features, however, can be discerned.

In the first place, the Commission gives considerable weight to the evaluation concerning the capacity to assume the obligations of the single market. This is not only because the single market is a central element of the *acquis* (coming therefore before areas such as agriculture or the structural funds in the list of contents of the Opinions) and is the centrepiece of the preaccession strategy. It is also because the applicant countries had already received clear indications, in the White Paper on the single market, of the precise steps necessary for the adjustment of their legislation for compliance with the *acquis*; and so in this area, more than in others, it was reasonable to assess future prospects on the basis of progress achieved. The Opinions include, in fact, a table showing in quantitative terms the number of measures for which by June 1997 each country had notified to the Commission 'the existence of adopted legislation having some degree of compatibility with the corresponding White Paper measures', compared with the total number of 899 regulations and directives cited in the White Paper. This quantitative analysis is, naturally, qualified by an assessment of each country's qualitative progress in the 'general evaluation' which figures in the chapter on the single market.

In the second place, the Commission's analyses show that the number of areas of the *acquis* where the 'medium-term' evaluation shows 'no significant difficulty' are rather few compared with those where 'substantial efforts will be needed', and it is accordingly more difficult to make judgments on the relative positions of the countries. Typically in the Opinions, the sectors of environment, transport, energy and agriculture all require 'reinforced measures', 'substantial efforts', or 'fundamental reform'. In the chapter on the environment, in particular, the formulations used in the conclusions reveal the difficulties encountered by the Commission's experts in assessing future compliance with the *acquis*; in fact, the 'medium term' (five years) is simply not sufficient here, and the time horizon extends into the 'long term' and 'very long term'. Even for the Czech Republic, at the positive end of the spectrum: 'transposition of the environmental *acquis* as well as compliance with important elements should be achieved in the medium term; however, effective compliance with a number of pieces of legislation

requiring a sustained high level of investment and considerable administrative effort could be achieved only in the long term'. For Romania:
'if it places higher priority on environmental issues, and significantly
increases financial and other resources, transposition of the *acquis*
could be achieved in the medium to long term; however, effective compliance with a number of pieces of legislation...could be achieved only
in the very long term'.

4. *Administrative Capacity*

This section of the Opinions examines the state of the public administration in each country, including relevant aspects of the judicial system, and assesses the current and prospective ability of the country to
carry out the functions required of a modern, democratic state with a
particular focus on the need to administer matters related to the *acquis*.

Effectively, this section completes the more general remarks on the
executive and the judiciary which are found in the earlier section on the
political criteria of membership, by giving more details of the organization and structure of the civil service. It describes the ministries
involved in the implementation of key areas of the *acquis*, including the
single market, competition, telecommunications, taxation, agriculture,
transport, employment and social policy, regional policy, environment,
consumer protection, justice and home affairs, customs, and financial
control. In many cases there are indications of the numbers of staff
employed, although the emphasis is on the quality rather than the
quantity of the administration. This survey is a remarkable effort to
describe and evaluate the situation, for the first time on a comparable
basis for all the ten countries, and has been widely appreciated as a
point of reference on which reforms can be based.

The leitmotiv of this section is indeed the need for continuing
reforms, in all the applicant countries, to strengthen administrative
capacity. This may be illustrated by examples from the Opinions on
Slovenia, a country whose administrative capacity is considered to be
relatively good, but which is nevertheless the object of many recommendations for reform. In the case of Slovenia, it is stated in general
that 'the civil service is understaffed in a number of key departments.
Although it has expanded and continues to do so the intake of graduates
is limited to a small base; there are serious shortages at middle and
senior management levels. These problems will have important
negative consequences for the ability of the civil service to function

effectively, unless they are successfully addressed in the near future.' In the case of specific ministries in Slovenia, there are numerous remarks of the following kind: 'due to a large turnover of staff, resulting partly from trained staff being recruited by the private sector, it is difficult to assess the capacities of existing staff; it will be necessary to consolidate professional standards, including training measures and improvements in pay' (Ministry of Finance). Again: 'the administrative arrangements are at an early stage of development, the situation concerning financial control is not satisfactory, the effective administration of the *acquis* in this area [regional policy and cohesion] will require significant efforts to create an appropriate institutional, administrative and budgetary framework' (Ministry of Economic Relations and Development). And so on, for many other areas of administration, in all the applicant countries.

An important problem mentioned in this section of the Opinions is corruption; but because of the extraordinary difficulty of defining, measuring, and analysing this phenomenon in the public service—a difficulty not limited to the countries of Central and Eastern Europe—the Opinions do no more than mention it, in extremely guarded and diplomatic terms. To quote an example, again from the Opinion on Slovenia: 'public confidence in the civil service is variable; there is no evidence of significant corruption'.

The section concludes with a general evaluation, exhorting all the countries to undertake administrative reform.

Summaries and Conclusions

Each Opinion concludes with a 'summary and conclusion', reproduced below. These summaries are the versions of the Opinions which are most widely known, and in general faithfully reflect the full text: for example, in the case of the political and economic criteria, the summaries simply reproduce the 'general evaluations' which appear at the end of the relevant sections. But it should be borne in mind that the basis for the Commission's conclusions and recommendations was the full text of the Opinions; the 'executive summaries' were compiled only in the last stages of the exercise, and were not (as is sometimes the case with such reports!) the point of departure which determined the rest of the exercise; it was, indeed, for this reason that they were placed firmly at the end of the Opinions and not at the beginning.

The paragraphs of the 'conclusion' are of a standard form: a brief statement of the Commission's evaluations concerning the political criteria, the economic criteria, the *acquis*, and the administrative capacity, followed by a standard formula: 'In the light of these considerations, the Commission recommends that negotiations for accession should be opened with [Hungary, Poland, Estonia, the Czech Republic, Slovenia]' or 'In the light of these considerations, the Commission recommends that negotiations for accession should be opened with [Romania, Slovakia, Latvia, Lithuania, Bulgaria] as soon as they have made sufficient progress in satisfying the conditions of membership defined by the European Council in Copenhagen.'

Formally, therefore, the Commission submitted negative Opinions on none of the applicant countries. In the case of the five countries which were judged to be better prepared, it recommended the opening of negotiations, implicitly at the same time as Cyprus, for which the European Council had already decided to commence negotiations six months after the Intergovernmental Conference. In the case of the other five applicant countries, it recommended to open negotiations at a later date, in effect to be decided by the European Council in the light of the Commission's reports on progress.

To underline its non-discriminatory approach, the Commission concluded all the Opinions with an identical paragraph, indicating that the preaccession strategy and the reports apply to all ten applicant countries: 'The reinforced preaccession strategy will help [the country concerned] to prepare itself better to meet the obligations of membership, and to take action to improve the shortcomings identified in the Opinions. The Commission will present a report no later than the end of 1998 on the progress that [the country concerned] has achieved.'

The summaries which follow are presented not in alphabetic order, or according to a geographic grouping, but according to the chronological order of the countries' requests for membership. This was the approach which the Commission followed strictly in its presentation of the Opinions, and in Agenda 2000 to demonstrate its objective and non-discriminatory approach to the exercise. Once again, it is recalled that these summaries are highly condensed versions of longer texts: the Commission has made it clear in response to criticisms that the summaries contain misleading passages (for example, incomplete economic data) that it was the full texts of the Opinions, not the summaries, which provided the bases for its conclusions concerning the applicant countries. The sequence follows the chronological date of applications for membership (see Table 1.1).

Hungary

1. *Political Criteria*

Hungary's political institutions function properly. They respect the limits on their competences and cooperate with each other. Elections are free and fair and led to alternation of power in 1990 and 1994. The opposition plays a normal part in the operation of the institutions.

There are no major problems over respect for fundamental rights. The rights of minorities are guaranteed and protected. Certain improvements are still needed in the operation of the judicial system and in protection for the Roma, but the measures recently taken by the government constitute progress. The fight against corruption needs further reinforcement.

Hungary presents the characteristics of a democracy with stable institutions guaranteeing the rule of law, human rights and respect for and protection of minorities.

2. *Economic Criteria*

After a fall in GDP of nearly 20 per cent between 1989 and 1993, Hungary has seen renewed growth since 1994 (1.5 per cent in 1995, 1 per cent in 1996). This has been accompanied by progress towards stabilization of public finances, external accounts and inflation (19.8 per cent in 1996). Hungary has 10.2 million inhabitants and its GDP per capita is equivalent to 37 per cent of the EU average. 8 per cent of the working population are employed in the agricultural sector which contributes 7 per cent of gross value added. Trade with the EU has grown considerably since 1989 and now [1997] represents 60 per cent of Hungary's external trade.

On the basis of its analysis the Commission's judgment as to Hungary's ability to meet the economic criteria established at Copenhagen is as follows:

Hungary can be regarded as a functioning market economy. Liberalization and privatization have progressed considerably, and there has been strong growth of new private firms. In order to guarantee longer-term stability, the reform of pensions and social security needs to advance rapidly. The proposed method of pension reform would have the added benefit of deepening capital markets.

Hungary should be well able to cope with competitive pressure and market forces within the Union in the medium term, provided the macroeconomic conditions for strong investment growth remain in place. Hungarian enterprises are already competitive in EU markets. Restructuring of industry and banks is well underway. Hungary's record of consistent commitment to steady market reforms and its ability to take difficult decisions when they are necessary is an important positive factor. It has had a consistently high level of foreign direct investment. However, the key task is now to avoid unsustainable budgetary or external deficits, which hinder investment and restructuring, and halt the recent acceleration of growth.

3. *Capacity to Take on the Obligations of Membership*

Hungary has met the bulk of its obligations under the Europe Agreement, and the timetable set out in the Agreement has been met. The Agreement has functioned very well and it has been possible to resolve any bilateral difficulties which have arisen, in particular in the field of trade. Hungary has achieved a good rate of transposition of the rules and directives set out in the White Paper.

For the whole field related to the single market, and in particular competition, public procurement, intellectual property, company and accounting law, taxation, product liability, financial services, the legislative foundation is almost completely in place. Despite the efforts undertaken, the progress made in transposing legislation still needs to be accompanied by concrete measures of implementation, as well as establishment of an effective administrative underpinning. Hungary has some instruments which operate correctly (for instance in the field of public procurement, appeal procedures set out in the directives are applied and court cases have been started) but substantial efforts are still needed in a number of sectors, notably standardization.

As for the other parts of the *acquis*, Hungary should not have difficulty in applying it in the medium term, provided it continues its current preparation for accession in the following fields: education, training and youth; research and technological development; telecommunications; audiovisual; small and medium enterprises; international trade relations, and development.

By contrast substantial efforts will be needed for Hungary to be able to apply the *acquis* in consumer protection and customs controls.

Given the extent of restructuring and modernization efforts undertaken so far, there are good reasons to expect that most sectors of Hungarian industry in the medium term can be competitive operators in the single market.

For the environment, very important efforts will be needed, including massive investment and strengthening of administrative capacity for enforcement of legislation. Full compliance with the *acquis* could only be expected in the long to very long term and would necessitate increased levels of public expenditure.

Hungary has already made considerable progress on taking on the transport *acquis*. If it continues its efforts on road transport and technical controls this sector should not pose significant difficulties. Hungary will need to provide the investment necessary to extend the European transport network in order to ensure effective operation of the single market.

Hungary should also be able in the medium term to apply the *acquis* on employment and social affairs but efforts are still needed to improve the health system and apply EU health and safety at work standards. Hungary already has an effective labour inspectorate.

For regional policy Hungary has adopted a regional development policy which, if implemented, should permit it in the medium term to apply Community rules and make effective use of structural funds. Hungary will also need the necessary financial control instruments.

In the agriculture sector if progress is made in the veterinary and phytosanitary fields, and if the structures needed in the agrifood sector and for applying the CAP are reinforced, membership in the medium term should not pose significant problems for Hungary in applying the CAP in an appropriate manner.

For energy efforts are still needed in respect of monopoly operations, price fixing, access to networks and state intervention in the solid fuel and uranium sectors. Hungary has a nuclear power station at Paks which produces nearly 40 per cent of the country's electricity. It needs to modernize this in the medium term in order to bring it up into internationally accepted safety standards. It will also need to find a solution for nuclear waste.

On the basis of the analysis of its capacity to apply the *acquis*, Hungary could be in a position in the medium term to take and implement the measures necessary for removal of controls at its borders and establishment of these at the Union's external border.

Hungary should be in a position to participate at the appropriate time in the third stage of economic and monetary union, which implies coordination of economic policy and complete liberalization of capital movements. But it is premature to judge whether Hungary will be in a position, by the time of its accession, to participate in the Euro area. That will depend on how far the success of its structural transformation enables it to achieve and sustain permanently the convergence criteria. These are, however, not a condition for membership.

Hungary should be able to meet the justice and home affairs *acquis* in the next few years, even though particular attention will need to be paid to frontier controls, treatment of asylum seekers, visa policy and the fight against organized crime. Hungary has indicated a wish to join the Schengen Agreements.

Hungary should be able to fulfil its obligations in respect of the Common Foreign and Security Policy.

In addition, Hungary has reinforced its relations with its neighbours since 1989, and has signed Friendship and Good Neighbourliness Agreements with them recognizing existing frontiers and resolving almost all the potential disputes with them. It has played an important role in regional stability.

4. *Administrative and Legal Capacity*

If Hungary pursues the administrative reforms which have already been started, the necessary structures could be in place in the medium term to apply the *acquis* effectively.

The capacity of the judicial system to ensure uniform application of Community law is of great importance, particularly for the implementation of the single market. If Hungary pursues its efforts, the judicial system should be capable of applying Community law in the medium term.

Conclusion

In the light of these considerations, the Commission concludes that:

- Hungary presents the characteristics of a democracy, with stable institutions guaranteeing the rule of law, human rights and respect for and protection of minorities;
- Hungary can be regarded as a functioning market economy and it should be able to cope with competitive pressure and market forces within the Union in the medium term;
- if Hungary continues its efforts on transposition of the *acquis* relating particularly to the single market, and intensifies its work on its implementation, Hungary should become capable in the medium term of applying it fully. In addition, particular efforts will be needed to meet the *acquis* in sectors such as environment, customs control and energy. More generally, further administrative reform will be indispensable if Hungary is to have the structures to apply and enforce the *acquis* effectively.

In the light of these considerations, the Commission recommends that negotiations for accession should be opened with Hungary.

The reinforced preaccession strategy will help Hungary to prepare itself better to meet the obligations of membership, and to take action to improve the shortcomings identified in the Opinions. The Commission will present a report no later than the end of 1998 on the progress Hungary has achieved.

Poland

1. *Political Criteria*

Poland's political institutions function properly and in conditions of stability. They respect the limits on their competences and cooperate with each other. Legislative elections in 1991 and 1993, and presidential elections in 1995, were free and fair. In 1993 and 1995, when they led to alternation of power, this was properly achieved. The opposition plays a normal part in the operation of the institutions. Efforts to improve the operation of the judicial system and to intensify the fight against corruption will need to be sustained.

There are no major problems over respect for fundamental rights. There are, however, certain limitations to freedom of the press. Particular attention will be needed to how a new law limiting access to public service for certain categories of persons is implemented. Poland needs to complete procedures for compensating those whose property was seized by the Nazis or Communists.

Poland presents the characteristics of a democracy, with stable institutions guaranteeing the rule of law, human rights and respect for and protection of minorities.

2. *Economic Criteria*

Before 1989 the Polish economy was suffering seriously from stagnation, inflation and its foreign debt burden. The recovery plan initiated in January 1990 was drastic, but provoked only a limited drop in output (though output had already fallen substantially in the 1980s). By 1992 positive growth had already started, and has continued since (6.0 per cent in 1996). The budget deficit has been reduced to below 3 per cent of GDP; and the debt-servicing burden, after rescheduling was agreed in 1991, is being steadily reduced. Inflation rates have declined over recent years, but still stood at 19.9 per cent in 1996. GDP per head is about 31 per cent of the EU average, for a population of 38.6 million. The agricultural sector employed 27 per cent of the labour force in 1995, and accounted for 6.6 per cent of Gross Value Added. 70 per cent of Poland's exports are directed to the EU, and 65 per cent of its imports originate in the EU.

On the basis of its analysis, the Commission's judgment as to Poland's ability to meet the economic criteria established at Copenhagen is as follows:

Poland can be regarded as a functioning market economy. Prices and trade have been liberalized to a large extent. The economy has been successfully stabilized. Commitment to this policy line has been maintained through various changes in government. In order to guarantee longer-term stability, pension and social security systems need to be reformed. Financial services are underdeveloped. The banking sector needs further reform.

Poland should be well able to cope with competitive pressure and market forces within the Union in the medium term, provided that it maintains the pace of restructuring and keeps the economy open. Growth and investment are strong, and the rise in unit labour costs in the manufacturing sector has been moderate.

Recently, inflows of foreign direct investment have accelerated. The main problem is that of the larger state-owned companies, where management failures in the face of foreign competition could have serious consequences. Agriculture needs to be modernized, and there have been some reversals in trade policy.

3. *Capacity to Take on the Obligations of Membership*

Poland has already implemented significant elements of the provisions of the Europe Agreement, and for the most part according to the timetable for implementation set out in it. Too many trade-related problems have arisen, though most of them have been able to be resolved. Poland has achieved a satisfactory rate of transposition of the rules and directives identified in the White Paper, though there is still a considerable amount of legislative work left to do.

In respect of provisions relating specifically to the single market, substantial progress has been made on intellectual property, company law, taxation, accounting, and financial services. Work is still needed on public procurement, data protection, competition and liberalization of capital movements.

Notwithstanding the efforts which have been made, the progress made in transposing legislation still needs to be accompanied by concrete measures of implementation, as well as establishment of an effective administrative underpinning. Overall, the administrative infrastructure is either well established or recently set up and functioning normally. But the work of legislative adaptation is proceeding slowly in the field of technical rules and standards.

As for the other parts of the *acquis*, Poland should not have difficulty in applying it in the medium term in the following fields: education, training and youth; research and technological development; statistics; small and medium enterprises; development; and customs.

By contrast, substantial efforts will be needed for Poland to be able to apply the *acquis* in the fields of telecommunications; fisheries; and consumer protection. Polish industry is characterized by the existence of both a dynamic new private sector which should be able to compete in the single market in the medium term, and large sectors, mostly state owned, which need restructuring in order to be able to compete.

For the environment, very substantial efforts will be needed, including massive investment and strengthening of administrative capacity to enforce legislation. Full compliance with the *acquis* could be expected only in the long term, and would require increased levels of public expenditure.

For transport, Poland made notable progress in taking on the *acquis*, but considerable effort and investment will be needed in road transport. Provided that these efforts are made, the transport sector should not pose major problems in the medium term. But investment will be needed to extend the European transport network so as to ensure that the single market functions well.

In order to achieve the employment and social affairs *acquis* in the medium term, work is needed to adapt legislation in the field of health and safety at work.

In the field of regional policy and cohesion, if Poland implements the recommendations of its Task Force for Regional Policy, this will be a major step towards achieving the *acquis*. Given the necessary administrative framework, and the substantial improvement needed in the field of financial control, Poland should be able in the medium term to use the Union's regional and structural funds for its development effectively.

For agriculture, particular efforts will be needed to establish a coherent structural and rural development policy, and to implement veterinary and phytosanitary requirements and to strengthen the administrative structures necessary to apply the common agricultural policy. Provided these targets can be met, the common agricultural policy could be applied in an appropriate manner on accession in the medium term, although a solution to Poland's structural problems will require a long-term approach.

On energy, Poland has no nuclear power programme, and should have no difficulty in complying with the Euratom provisions. Poland should be able to comply with the rest of the energy *acquis* in the medium term, but this will require work on issues such as energy pricing, import barriers for oil products and state intervention in the coal sector.

On the basis of the analysis of its capacity to apply the *acquis*, Poland could be in a position in the medium term to take and implement the measures necessary for removal of controls at its borders with Member States of the Union.

Poland's participation in the third stage of economic and monetary union, which implies coordination of economic policy and complete liberalization of capital movements, should pose no problems in the medium term. But it is premature to judge whether Poland will be in a position, by the time of its accession, to participate in the Euro area. That will depend on how far the success of its structural transformation enables it to achieve and sustain permanently the convergence criteria. These are, however, not a condition for membership.

Poland faces significant challenges in the field of justice and home affairs, particularly concerning drugs, border management and transnational crime. Provided that continuing efforts are made, Poland could be able to meet the requirements of the *acquis* in the next few years.

Poland should be able to fulfil its obligations in respect of the Common Foreign and Security Policy.

In addition, Poland has no territorial disputes with any member state or neighbouring candidate country. All its state frontiers are regulated by treaty.

4. *Administrative and Legal Capacity*

If Poland continues its comprehensive reform efforts in this area it could achieve in the medium term the administrative structures necessary for the essential work of applying and enforcing the *acquis* effectively.

The same applies to Poland's judicial system, which has an equally important part to play.

Conclusion

In the light of these considerations, the Commission concludes that:

- Poland presents the characteristics of a democracy, with stable institutions guaranteeing the rule of law, human rights and respect for and protection of minorities;
- Poland can be regarded as a functioning market economy, and should be able to cope with competitive pressure and market forces within the Union in the medium term;
- if Poland continues its efforts on transposition of the *acquis* relating particularly to the single market, and intensifies work on its implementation, Poland should become able to participate fully in the single market in the medium term. Particular effort and investment will be needed to meet the *acquis* in sectors such as agriculture, environment and transport. Further administrative reform will be indispensable if Poland is to have the structures to apply and enforce the *acquis* effectively.

In the light of these considerations, the Commission recommends that negotiations for accession should be opened with Poland.

The reinforced preaccession strategy will help Poland to prepare itself better to meet the obligations of membership, and to take action to improve the shortcomings identified in this Opinion. The Commission will present a report no later than the end of 1998 on the progress Poland has achieved.

Romania

1. *Political Criteria*

Romania has democratic institutions whose stability now seems secure. They still need to be consolidated by fuller respect in practice for the rule of law at all levels of the structures of government. Elections are free and fair, and in November 1996 led to genuine alternation of power.

A number of gaps remain as regards respect for fundamental rights, even if the measures adopted and the undertakings given by the Romanian authorities since November 1996 constitute progress. Considerable efforts are still needed in the fight against corruption, and in order to improve the operation of the judicial system and the protection of individual rights against the police and the secret services as well as during the operation of the penal system.

If the Hungarian minority seems well integrated in the light of recent improvements in their situation, this does not seem to be the case for the Roma, who constitute a significant minority.

Reforms undertaken for protection of children placed in orphanages constitute significant progress, but still need to achieve their full results.

Current improvements following the arrival in power of a new government make it possible to conclude that Romania is on the way to satisfying the political criteria set by the European Council at Copenhagen.

2. *Economic Criteria*

After several earlier unsuccessful efforts at reform of the Romanian economy, the new government elected in November 1996 has put in place a radical programme of macroeconomic stabilization and structural reform. This policy is being implemented at a time of diminishing growth (7.1 per cent in 1995, 4.1 per cent in 1996), accelerating inflation (56.9 per cent in 1996) and deteriorating budget and trading deficits.

Romania has a population of 22.6 million and GDP per head is 24 per cent of the EU average. The agricultural sector employs more than one third of the working population and contributes 20 per cent of the gross value added. There are still substantial structural problems despite recent privatization. Trade with the EU represents 55 per cent of Romania's exports and 52 per cent of its imports.

On the basis of its analysis, the Commission's judgment as to Romania's ability to meet the economic criteria established at Copenhagen is as follows:

Romania has made considerable progress in the creation of a market economy. The reorientation of economic policy since the recent change of government has meant a change for the better, but much still needs to be done. While prices have been almost fully liberalized, property rights are not yet fully assured for land, the legal system is still fragile and policy-making on economic issues has not always been coherent. Further efforts to consolidate the administrative and legal framework and to address persistent macroeconomic imbalances are required to ensure a stable environment.

Romania would face serious difficulties in coping with competitive pressure and market forces within the Union in the medium term. It has made progress recently towards improving the competitive capacity of its economy, notably by addressing major distortions such as low energy prices, by accelerating privatization, and by beginning to liquidate large loss-making state owned firms. However, much of Romania's industry is obsolete and agriculture needs to be modernized. The low levels of research and development, and of skills among the workforce also suggest that the economy needs a number of years of sustained structural reform.

3. *Capacity to Take on the Obligations of Membership*

Romania has made significant efforts to comply with its obligations under the Europe Agreement and with the recommendations of the White Paper, but the rate of transposition is too low.

Romanian legislation has only taken on a small part of the *acquis* relating to the key elements of the single market including competition, except in respect of industrial and intellectual property. The scale of progress still needed requires very substantial and sustained efforts, both in approximation of legislation and in the creation of structures for implementing it. Complete restructuring of the financial sector, in order to re-establish essential public and investor confidence in it, is among the highest priorities.

In general, the weakness of public administration constitutes a serious problem, putting into question both the rate and the quality of approximation of legislation. The various structures necessary for applying legislation on the single market are not currently capable of carrying out their roles.

As for the other parts of the *acquis*, if Romania pursues its work of transposition, it should not have significant difficulty in applying it in the medium term in the following fields: education, training and youth; research and technological development; fisheries; small and medium enterprises; consumer protection; international trade relations; and development.

By contrast, substantial efforts will be needed in the fields of telecommunications; audiovisual; taxation and customs.

Romania has not yet created the conditions which are conducive to a dynamic and competitive private sector. Its industry therefore will only be ready in the long term to withstand competitive pressures in the single market.

For the environment, very important efforts will be needed, including massive investment and strengthening of administrative capacity for enforcement of legislation. Full compliance with the *acquis* could only be expected in the very long term and would necessitate increased levels of public expenditure.

Romania has made some progress in taking on the *acquis* for transport. It needs to increase its efforts, notably in respect of road freight transport and in the maritime and rail sectors. Romania will also need to provide the investment necessary to complete the European transport network, which is an essential element of the effective operation of the single market.

Romania still needs to make substantial efforts to bring its employment and social affairs standards into line with those of the EU. Progress is particularly needed in respect of labour law and health and safety. There also needs to be an effective labour inspectorate.

On regional policy Romania has barely started to put in place the structures needed to use effectively the Union's structural funds. It will also need to establish effective systems of financial control.

Romania needs to implement fundamental reform of its agricultural sector before it can fulfil the obligations of membership. Particular effort will be needed to restructure the sector and the agrifood industry and to put in place health and quality control mechanisms. Romania will also need to strengthen the administrative structures responsible for implementing the common agricultural policy.

For energy efforts are still needed on price-fixing, state intervention in the solid fuel and uranium sectors and the operation of monopolies. Romania has at Cernavoda a nuclear power station which produces around 8 per cent of the country's electricity. It was built in accordance with Western technology. A solution will need to be found to the problem of nuclear waste.

On the basis of the analysis of Romania's capacity to apply the *acquis*, it is not yet possible to be sure when it could become able to take and implement the measures necessary to remove the controls at borders between Romania and Member States of the Union and to establish them instead at the Union's external border.

Romania does not seem to be in a position to participate in the third stage of economic and monetary union which implies coordination of economic policies and the complete liberalization of movement of capital. It is premature to judge whether Romania will be in a position by the time of its accession to participate in the Euro area. That will depend on how far the success of its structural transformation enables it to achieve and sustain permanently the convergence criteria. These are however not a condition for membership.

Romania faces a particular challenge in justice and home affairs. So far it has made limited progress in taking on the *acquis* in this field. The new government has undertaken an ambitious programme to introduce the essential institutional reforms.

Romania should be able to fulfil its obligations in respect of the Common Foreign and Security Policy.

Romania has recently improved its relations with its neighbours particularly with Hungary and Ukraine, and has settled most of its disputes with these countries.

4. *Administrative and Legal Capacity*

Romania's administrative structures will need a major and sustained effort of reform if it is to have the capacity to apply the *acquis* effectively.

The capacity of the judicial system to ensure uniform application of

Community law is of great importance, especially for implementation of the single market. It is not yet possible to judge Romania's prospects in this sector.

Conclusion

In the light of these considerations, the Commission concludes that :

- the current improvement in Romania, following the arrival in power of a new government, indicates that Romania is on its way to satisfy the political criteria;
- Romania has made considerable progress in the creation of a market economy, but it would still face serious difficulties in coping with competitive pressure and market forces within the Union in the medium term;
- despite the progress that has been made, Romania has neither transposed nor taken on the essential elements of the *acquis*, particularly as regards the internal market. It is therefore uncertain whether Romania will be in a position to assume the obligations of membership in the medium term. In addition, considerable efforts will be needed in the areas of environment, transport, employment and social affairs, justice and home affairs as well as agriculture. More generally, substantial administrative reform will be indispensable if Romania is to have the structures to apply and enforce the *acquis* effectively.

In the light of these considerations, the Commission considers that negotiations for accession to the European Union should be opened with Romania as soon as it has made sufficient progress in satisfying the conditions of membership defined by the European Council in Copenhagen.

The reinforced preaccession strategy will help Romania to prepare itself better to meet the obligations of membership, and to take action to improve the shortcomings identified in the Opinions. The Commission will present a report no later than the end of 1998 on the progress Romania has achieved.

Slovakia

1. *Political Criteria*

Slovakia's situation presents a number of problems in respect of the criteria defined by the European Council in Copenhagen.

The operation of Slovakia's institutions is characterized by the fact that the government does not sufficiently respect the powers devolved by the constitution to other bodies and that it too often disregards the rights of the opposition. The constant tension between the government and the

President of the Republic is one example of this. Similarly, the way in which the government recently ignored the decisions of the Constitutional Court and the Central Referendum Commission on the occasion of the vote on 23/24 May 1997 directly threatened the stability of the institutions. The frequent refusal to involve the opposition in the operation of the institutions, particularly in respect of parliamentary control, reinforces this tendency.

In this context, the use made by the government of the police and the secret services is worrying. Substantial efforts need to be made to ensure fuller independence of the judicial system, so that it can function in satisfactory conditions. The fight against corruption needs to be pursued with greater effectiveness.

Apart from this the treatment of the Hungarian minority, which still lacks the benefit of a law on use of minority languages, even though the Slovak authorities had undertaken to adopt one, as envisaged by the constitution, needs to be improved. The situation of the Roma similarly needs attention from the authorities.

In the light of these elements, although the institutional framework defined by the Slovak constitution responds to the needs of a parliamentary democracy where elections are free and fair, nevertheless the situation is unsatisfactory both in terms of the stability of the institutions and of the extent to which they are rooted in political life. Despite recommendations made by the European Union in a number of demarches and declarations, there has been no noticeable improvement.

2. *Economic Criteria*

After a fall in GNP of nearly 25 per cent between 1989 and 1993 Slovakia has seen positive growth since 1994 which in 1995 and 1996 reached high levels (6.8 per cent in 1995, 6.9 per cent in 1996), while inflation has fallen (5.4 per cent in 1996). This has, however, been accompanied by an increase in budget deficits and in particular by a worsening of external accounts.

Slovakia has 5.4 million inhabitants and its GDP per capita is 41 per cent of the EU average. The agricultural sector employs nearly 10 per cent of the working population, and produces 6 per cent of gross value added. Trade relations with the EU have grown considerably since 1989 and now represent 36 per cent of Slovakia's imports and 41 per cent of its exports.

On the basis of this analysis, the Commission's judgment as to Slovakia's ability to meet the economic criteria established at Copenhagen is as follows:

Slovakia has introduced most of the reforms necessary to establish a market economy. The price system has been liberalized and allocation decisions are decentralized by the advanced privatization process. Nevertheless, a restrictive Price Law was introduced in 1996, and the draft

Enterprise Revitalization Act would be a major step back from market mechanisms. The financial sector needs to be reinforced, and progress is needed in the regulation of the bankruptcy process and capital markets.

Slovakia should be able to cope with competitive pressure and market forces within the Union in the medium term, but this would require more transparent and market-based policies. For a number of years, the economy has grown rapidly, with low inflation. The country has low wage costs and a skilled labour force. However, enterprise restructuring has been slow, which is gradually undermining economic growth and external balance. The low level of foreign direct investment reflects these structural problems, which need to be tackled swiftly and in a transparent way.

3. *Capacity to Take on the Obligations of Membership*

Slovakia has for the most part met its obligations under the Europe Agreement and mostly according to the timetable for implementation set out in it. The Agreement has operated in a satisfactory manner, but it has not been possible to resolve all the problems which have arisen in relation to both the democratic functioning of the institutions and commercial matters. In particular, the introduction by Slovakia of a system of import deposits is not in accordance with the Agreement. Slovakia has achieved a satisfactory rate of transposition of the rules and directives identified in the White Paper.

Significant progress has been achieved on transposing legislation related to key areas of the single market such as company law, banking, free movement of capital and taxation, even if further work is needed to achieve full alignment with EU rules. More substantial efforts are needed to apply the *acquis* in the medium term on standards and certification, industrial and intellectual property, competition, public procurement and insurance.

Notwithstanding the efforts which have been made, the progress made in transposing legislation still needs to be accompanied by concrete measures of implementation as well as establishment of an effective administrative underpinning. Slovakia has a number of instruments which operate correctly, but substantial efforts are still needed in some sectors, notably public procurement, industrial and intellectual property and standardization.

As for the other parts of the *acquis*, provided it continues its efforts, Slovakia should not have particular difficulty in applying it in the medium term in the following fields: education, training and youth; research and technological development; audiovisual; small and medium enterprises; consumer protection; international trade relations; and development.

By contrast, Slovakia will need to make substantial efforts in order to apply the *acquis* in the fields of telecommunications and customs.

The integration of Slovak industry in the European market could face difficulties to proceed satisfactorily over the medium term. This will require diversification away from heavy industries and more effective restructuring of enterprises.

For the environment, very important efforts will be needed, including massive investment and strengthening of administrative capacity for enforcement of legislation. Full compliance with the *acquis* could only be expected in the long to very long term.

Slovakia has made efforts towards applying the *acquis* in the field of transport. But further progress is needed on road freight transport and the railway sector, without which it would be hard for Slovakia to meet the obligations of accession. Only if the situation improves is the transport sector unlikely to pose major problems. Slovakia needs to make the necessary effort, in collaboration with the international financial institutions, to integrate itself into the European transport network and to achieve establishment of the TENs which are important elements in the effective functioning of the single market.

Slovakia still has substantial work to do to align its employment and social affairs standards on those of the EU. Progress is needed in particular on labour law, health and safety at work and the labour inspectorate, which does not currently have the autonomy necessary to fulfil its role properly.

As for regional policy and cohesion Slovakia needs to pay more attention to existing regional disparities, and also to establish the necessary financial controls, in order to apply Community rules and in due course utilize structural funds.

In agriculture, provided there is progress on veterinary and phytosanitary controls, on strengthening of the structures needed to apply CAP and on restructuring the agrifood sector, accession in the medium term should not cause significant problems for Slovakia in implementing the CAP in an appropriate manner.

As for energy, work is still needed on operation of monopolies, price fixing, access to networks and state intervention in the solid fuel sector. Slovakia has a nuclear power station at Bohunice which produces nearly 50 per cent of the country's electricity; and is constructing a new power station at Mochovce. It must in the medium term modernize two of the units at Bohunice to bring them up to internationally accepted safety standards; and must take the appropriate measures to close the units which cannot be modernized. A long-term solution needs to be found for nuclear waste.

On the basis of the analysis of its capacity to apply the *acquis* it is not yet possible to be sure when Slovakia could become able to take and implement the measures necessary to remove the controls at borders between Slovakia and Member States of the Union and to replace them at the Union's external border.

Slovakia's participation in the third stage of economic and monetary union, which implies coordination of economic policy and the complete liberalization of capital movements, could present some difficulties given the incompatibility of the rules governing the central bank with those of the EU, and also the need to restructure the banking sector. It is premature to judge whether Slovakia will be in a position by the time of its accession, to participate in the Euro area. That will depend on how far the success of its structural transformation enables it to achieve and sustain permanently the convergence criteria. These are however not a condition for membership.

Slovakia should be able to apply the *acquis* on justice and home affairs in the medium term, though particular attention needs to be given to frontier controls, visa policy and the fight against organized crime. Progress in this sector will also depend on respect for fundamental democratic rights.

Slovakia should be able to fulfil its obligations in respect of the Common Foreign and Security Policy.

Since 1989 Slovakia has strengthened its relations with its neighbours and settled almost all its disputes with them.

4. *Administrative and Legal Capacity*

If Slovakia undertakes substantial efforts to reform its administration, the necessary structures could be in place in the medium term to apply the *acquis* effectively.

The capacity of the judicial system to ensure correct and uniform application of Community law is important, particularly for achievement of the single market. In current circumstances it is difficult to judge Slovakia's progress in this field.

Conclusion

In the light of these considerations, the Commission concludes that Slovakia does not fulfil in a satisfying manner the political conditions set out by the European Council in Copenhagen, because of the instability of Slovakia's institutions, their lack of rootedness in political life and the shortcomings in the functioning of its democracy.

This situation is so much more regrettable since Slovakia could satisfy the economic criteria in the medium term and is firmly committed to take on the *acquis*, particularly concerning the internal market even if further progress is still required to ensure the effective application of the *acquis*.

In the light of these considerations, the Commission considers that negotiations for accession to the European Union should be opened with Slovakia as soon as it has made sufficient progress in satisfying the conditions of membership defined by the European Council in Copenhagen.

The reinforced preaccession strategy will help Slovakia to prepare itself better to meet the obligations of membership, and to take action to improve the shortcomings identified in the Opinions. The Commission will present a report no later than the end of 1998 on the progress Slovakia has achieved.

Latvia

1. Political Criteria

Latvia's political institutions function properly and in conditions of stability. They respect the limits on their competences and cooperate with each other. Elections in 1992 and 1995 were free and fair, and in each case permitted the establishment of coalition governments. The opposition plays a normal part in the operation of the institutions. Efforts to improve the operation of the judicial system and to intensify the fight against corruption need to be sustained.

There are no major problems over respect for fundamental rights. But Latvia needs to take measures to accelerate naturalization procedures to enable the Russian speaking non-citizens to become better integrated into Latvian society. It should also pursue its efforts to ensure equality of treatment for non-citizens and minorities, in particular for access to professions and participation in the democratic process.

Latvia demonstrates the characteristics of a democracy, with stable institutions guaranteeing the rule of law and human rights.

2. Economic Criteria

In the first three years after independence Latvia's output declined by 50 per cent. First signs of recovery in 1994 were undermined by a banking and budget crisis the following year; but growth turned positive again in 1996 (2.8 per cent). Since 1995 the current government has conducted a tight fiscal policy, though revenue collection is still a problem. The foreign debt ratio remains low, but Latvia has a high trade deficit. Inflation rates have declined over recent years, but still stood at 17.6 per cent in 1996. GDP per head is about 18 per cent of the EU average, for a population of 2.5 million. The agricultural sector employs 18 per cent of the labour force, and accounts for 9.9 per cent of gross value added. 45 per cent of Latvia's exports are directed to the EU, and 50 per cent of its imports originate in the EU.

On the basis of its analysis, the Commission's judgment as to Latvia's ability to meet the economic criteria established at Copenhagen is as follows:

Latvia has made considerable progress in creating a market economy. Trade and prices have largely been liberalized. Much headway has been made in stabilizing the economy. While there has been significant progress in establishing the legislative framework, effective implementation is lagging behind. Also, not all the necessary regulatory bodies are in place or working properly. Privatization is not complete; the remaining state-owned companies are generally in poor financial condition and there is a shortage of investors.

Latvia would face serious difficulties in coping with competitive pressure and market forces within the Union in the medium term. The Latvian economy is relatively open and labour costs are low. However, exports consist mainly of low value-added goods. Industrial restructuring, as well as enterprise restructuring, is still needed. The banking sector is underdeveloped and weak in parts. Agriculture needs to be modernized.

3. *Capacity to Take on the Obligations of Membership*

Even before the Europe Agreement has entered into force, Latvia has made significant efforts to comply with some of the obligations which will come into effect with it. Latvia is meeting its obligations under the Free Trade Agreement, and according to the timetable for implementation set out in it. No serious bilateral problems have arisen. Latvia has also made some efforts towards compliance with the essential single market legislation. It has made progress in the areas of banking, industrial property rights, conformity assessment and standards and commercial law. But further work needs to be done on intellectual property rights, public markets, personal data, competition (especially the transparency of state aids), taxation and other areas.

A problem for further progress may be the weakness of the Latvian public administration, which affects not only the pace of approximation of legislation but also the quality of its implementation and enforcement.

As for the other parts of the *acquis*, Latvia should not have significant difficulty in applying it in the medium term in the following fields: education, training and youth; research and technological development; telecommunications; audiovisual; fisheries; small and medium enterprises; trade and international economic relations; and development.

By contrast, substantial efforts will be needed in the fields of statistics and customs.

Provided that Latvia maintains current positive trends towards industrial restructuring, its industry should be able to cope with integration into the single market in the medium term.

For the environment, very substantial efforts will be needed, including massive investment and strengthening of administrative capacity to enforce legislation. Full compliance with the *acquis* could only be expected in the long term and would require increased levels of public expenditure.

Latvia has made real progress in the field of transport, especially air transport. Provided efforts are made in road transport, rail and sea transport, no major problems are to be expected in applying the *acquis* relating to the single market. But investment will be needed to extend the European transport network so as to ensure that the single market functions well.

It should be possible for Latvia to achieve the employment and social affairs *acquis* in the medium term, provided that Latvia makes substantial efforts to adapt its legislation to EU requirements in fields such as health and safety and labour law.

Latvia has opted to pursue its regional policy within the framework of its national development strategy. Given the necessary administrative reforms, and establishment in parallel of effective systems of financial control, Latvia should become able to use the Union's regional and structural funds for its development effectively.

The agriculture sector needs restructuring, and only a limited number of the mechanisms of the common agricultural policy currently exist. A substantial and sustained effort will be required to prepare for accession in the medium term.

In the energy field, Latvia has no nuclear power programme, and no difficulties are foreseen for Latvian compliance with Euratom provisions. But work will be needed to prepare to meet the *acquis* in the fields of energy pricing, access to networks, energy efficiency and environmental norms.

On the basis of the analysis of Latvia's capacity to apply the *acquis*, it is not yet possible to be sure when it could become able to take and implement the measures necessary to remove the controls at borders between Latvia and Member States of the Union.

Latvia's participation in the third stage of economic and monetary union, which implies coordination of economic policy and complete liberalization of capital movements, still poses problems in the medium term. It is premature to judge whether Latvia will be in a position, by the time of its accession, to participate in the Euro area. That will depend on how far the success of its structural transformation enables it to achieve and sustain permanently the convergence criteria. These are, however, not a condition for membership.

In the field of justice and home affairs, Latvia is starting from a low base and faces considerable difficulties in preparing itself. A major and sustained effort will be needed if Latvia is to be ready to meet the *acquis* in the medium term.

Latvia should be able to fulfil its obligations in respect of the Common Foreign and Security Policy.

In addition, Latvia has no major territorial disputes with any Member State or candidate country. Latvia has set development of good relations with Russia as a major priority of its foreign policy, and has achieved important progress.

4. *Administrative and Legal Capacity*

For Latvia to have in the medium term the administrative structures necessary for the essential work of applying and enforcing the *acquis* effectively, there will need to be a major, reinforced effort of reform.

The same applies to Latvia's judicial system, which has an equally important role to play.

Conclusion

In the light of these considerations, the Commission concludes that:

- Latvia presents the characteristics of a democracy, with stable institutions, guaranteeing the rule of law, human rights and respect for and protection of minorities. But measures need to be taken to accelerate the rate of naturalization of Russian-speaking non-citizens to enable them to become better integrated into Latvian society;
- Latvia has made considerable progress in the creation of a market economy, but it would face serious difficulties in coping with competitive pressure and market forces within the Union in the medium term;
- Latvia has made some progress in transposing and implementing the *acquis* relating particularly to the single market. With considerable further effort it should become able to participate fully in the single market in the medium term. Particular efforts, including investment, will be needed to apply the *acquis* fully in sectors such as environment and agriculture. Strengthening of the administrative structure is indispensable if Latvia is to have the structures to apply and enforce the *acquis* effectively.

In the light of these considerations, the Commission considers that negotiations for accession to the European Union should be opened with Latvia as soon as it has made sufficient progress in satisfying the conditions of membership defined by the European Council in Copenhagen.

The reinforced preaccession strategy will help Latvia to prepare itself better to meet the obligations of membership, and to take action to improve the shortcomings identified in this Opinion. The Commission will present a report no later than the end of 1998 on the progress Latvia has achieved.

Estonia

1. *Political Criteria*

Estonia's political institutions function properly and in conditions of stability. They respect the limits on their competences and cooperate with each other. Elections in 1992 and 1995 were free and fair, and in the latter case led to an alternation of power. The opposition plays a normal part in the operation of the institutions. Efforts to improve the operation of the judicial system and to intensify the fight against corruption need to be sustained.

There are no major problems over respect for fundamental rights. But Estonia needs to take measures to accelerate naturalization procedures to enable the Russian-speaking non-citizens to become better integrated into Estonian society.

Estonia presents the characteristics of a democracy, with stable institutions guaranteeing the rule of law and human rights.

2. *Economic Criteria*

After a sharp contraction of output immediately following independence, the economy has been growing since the second half of 1993 (4.0 per cent in 1996). The government has more or less maintained a principle of balanced budgets in public finances. External debt is low, though Estonia runs a high trade deficit. Inflation rates have declined over recent years, but still stood at 23.1 per cent in 1996. GDP per head is about 23 per cent of the EU average, for a population of 1.5 million. The agricultural sector employs 8 per cent of the labour force, and accounts for 7 per cent of gross value added. 54 per cent of Estonia's exports are directed to the EU, and 66 per cent of its imports originate in the EU.

On the basis of its analysis, the Commission's judgment as to Estonia's ability to meet the economic criteria established at Copenhagen is as follows:

Estonia can be regarded as a functioning market economy. It has liberalized foreign trade and privatized the public sector. Prices have been liberalized to a very large extent. The currency board system and the prudent fiscal stance have helped to reduce inflation. The legislative framework is largely in place. But land reform has been slow, and reform of the pension system has not yet started.

Estonia should be able to make the progress necessary to cope with competitive pressures and market forces within the Union in the medium term, provided in particular that the export base is broadened. The setting of a low exchange rate and low unit labour cost have facilitated the switch to light manufacturing industry as a source of foreign reserves. The banking sector is healthy and expanding strongly. Estonia has been a major recipient of foreign direct investment, although the inflow has decreased recently. But the export base is rather narrow, and the need to finance rising trade and current account deficits is a matter for concern.

3. *Capacity to Take on the Obligations of Membership*

Estonia has already made serious efforts to apply some of the obligations which will come into effect with the Europe Agreement, even before this has entered into force. It is meeting its obligations under the Free Trade

Agreement, and according to the timetable for implementation set out in it. No serious bilateral problems have arisen. Estonia has also adopted significant elements of the *acquis* relating to the single market, and has made a good start in transposing the rules and directives set out in the White Paper. In the fields of company law, accounting, data protection and capital liberalization, it is well on the way to putting in place the necessary legislative foundation. There is still substantial work to be done on public procurement, intellectual property, financial services, taxation and competition (especially the transparency of state aids).

Despite the progress achieved in the field of legislation, there are doubts about the capacity of the Estonian administration to implement this legal framework. But the present significant weaknesses should be temporary, given the high quality of existing staff.

As for the other aspects of the *acquis*, Estonia should not have difficulty in applying it in the medium term in the following fields: education, training and youth; research and technological development; audiovisual; small and medium enterprises; trade and international economic relations; and development.

By contrast, substantial efforts will be needed in the fields of statistics; fisheries; consumer protection; and customs.

Estonia has made good progress in industrial restructuring. Provided that current efforts are maintained, its industry should be able to cope with integration into the single market in the medium term.

Estonia has moved quickly to liberalize its telecommunications. Provided that current efforts at liberalization and transposition of laws are maintained, it should be able to apply the *acquis* in the medium term.

For the environment, very substantial efforts will be needed, including massive investment and strengthening of administrative capacity to enforce legislation. Partial compliance with the *acquis* could be achieved in the medium term. Full compliance could be achieved only in the long term.

Estonia has made progress in taking on the *acquis* in the transport sector, but needs to make improvements in the road freight and maritime sectors, and pay particular attention to safety issues. Provided this is achieved, accession in the medium term should not pose major problems. But investment will be needed to extend the European transport network so as to ensure that the single market functions well.

It should be possible for Estonia to apply the employment and social affairs *acquis* in the medium term, provided that it works to align its legislation with EU standards e.g. for health and safety and labour law.

In the field of regional policy and cohesion, provided that Estonia creates the necessary administrative and budgetary framework, and takes the steps necessary to create adequate structures of financial control, it should be able in the medium term to use regional and structural funds to support its development effectively.

The agriculture sector needs restructuring, and only a limited number of the mechanisms of the common agricultural policy presently exist. A substantial effort will be needed to prepare for accession in the medium term.

In the field of energy, Estonia has no nuclear energy programme, so no difficulties are foreseen for Estonia to comply with Euratom provisions. Estonia should be able to comply with most of the energy *acquis* in the medium term, provided that work is maintained on monopolies, access to networks, energy pricing and restructuring of the oil shale industry.

On the basis of the analysis of Estonia's capacity to apply the *acquis*, it is not yet possible to be sure when it could become able to take and implement the measures necessary to remove the controls at borders between Estonia and Member States of the Union.

Estonia's participation in the third stage of economic and monetary union, which implies coordination of economic policy and complete liberalization of capital movements, should pose few problems in the medium term. It is premature to judge whether Estonia will be in a position, by the time of its accession, to participate in the Euro area. That will depend on how far the success of its structural transformation enables it to achieve and sustain permanently the convergence criteria. These are, however, not a condition for membership.

In justice and home affairs, Estonia has started from a low base and made encouraging progress, notably in the field of border control. But a major, sustained effort will be needed if it is to meet the *acquis* in the medium term.

Estonia should be able to fulfil its obligations in respect of the Common Foreign and Security Policy.

In addition, Estonia has no territorial disputes with Member States or neighbouring candidate countries. Estonia gives high priority to its relationship with Russia, and has achieved important progress, though there is still no border agreement between them.

4. *Administrative and Legal Capacity*

For Estonia to have in the medium term the administrative structures necessary for the essential work of applying and enforcing the *acquis* effectively, there will need to be a major effort of reform.

It is not yet possible to judge when Estonia's judicial system, which has an equally important role to play, will acquire the capacity to play it effectively, even though Estonia has recently undertaken an extensive programme of recruitment of new judges.

Conclusion

In the light of these considerations, the Commission concludes that:

- Estonia presents the characteristics of a democracy, with stable institutions guaranteeing the rule of law, human rights and respect for and protection of minorities. But measures need to be taken to accelerate naturalization of Russian-speaking non-citizens, to enable them to become better integrated into Estonian society;
- Estonia can be regarded as a functioning market economy, and it should be able to make the progress necessary to cope with competitive pressure and market forces within the Union in the medium term;
- Estonia has made considerable progress in transposing and implementing the *acquis* relating particularly to the single market. With further effort it should become able to participate fully in the single market in the medium term. Particular efforts, including investment, will be needed to apply the *acquis* fully in sectors such as environment. Strengthening of the administrative structure will be indispensable if Estonia is to have the structures to apply and enforce the *acquis* effectively.

In the light of these recommendations, the Commission recommends that negotiations for accession should be opened with Estonia.

The reinforced preaccession strategy will help Estonia to prepare itself better to meet the obligations of membership, and to take action to improve the shortcomings identified in this Opinion. The Commission will present a report no later than the end of 1998 on the progress Estonia has achieved.

Lithuania

1. *Political Criteria*

Lithuania's political institutions function properly and in conditions of stability. They respect the limits on their competences and cooperate with each other. Elections in 1992 and 1996 were free and fair, and in each case permitted an alternation of power in proper conditions. The opposition plays a normal part in the operation of the institutions. Efforts to improve the operation of the judicial system and to intensify the fight against corruption need to be sustained.

There are no major problems over respect for fundamental rights.

Lithuania demonstrates the characteristics of a democracy, with stable institutions guaranteeing the rule of law, human rights and respect for and protection of minorities.

2. *Economic Criteria*

In the first three years after independence there was a very serious decline in output. It was halted only by the introduction of a new currency and the establishment of a currency board in 1993/94. Since then there have been increasing rates of positive growth every year (3.6 per cent in 1996), despite the banking crisis in 1995. Despite reduced tax revenues, Lithuania has maintained a reasonably tight fiscal stance. Foreign debt is at modest levels, and the trade deficit is under control. Inflation is down from very high levels in 1992/93 to 24.6 per cent in 1996. GDP per head is about 24 per cent of the EU average, for a population of 3.7 million. The agricultural sector employs 24 per cent of the labour force, and accounts for 9 per cent of gross value added. The EU is Lithuania's largest trading partner, taking 37 per cent of total trade.

On the basis of its analysis, the Commission's judgment as to Lithuania's ability to meet the economic criteria established at Copenhagen is as follows:

Lithuania has made considerable progress in the creation of a market economy. Trade and prices have been largely liberalized, and considerable progress has been achieved in the area of macroeconomic stabilization. However, further progress is needed, particularly in the areas of relative price adjustments, large-scale privatization and bankruptcy proceedings. The main element still missing is the enforcement of financial discipline for enterprises.

Lithuania would face serious difficulties in coping with competitive pressure and market forces within the Union in the medium term. The marked recent improvement in policy would, if sustained, accelerate the establishment of a market economy and strengthen competitiveness. But substantial enterprise restructuring is still required. Agriculture needs to be modernized, and the banking sector is still weak.

3. *Capacity to Take on the Obligations of Membership*

Even before the Europe Agreement has entered into force, Lithuania has made significant efforts to comply with some of the obligations which will come into effect with it. It is meeting its obligations under the Free Trade Agreement, and according to the timetable for implementation set out in it. No serious bilateral problems have arisen. Lithuania has also made some progress towards compliance with the essential single market legislation. It has made progress in the areas of company law, data protection and accounting. But further work needs to be done on intellectual property rights, public markets, liberalization of capital markets, financial services, taxation, competition and other areas.

A problem for further progress may be the weakness of the Lithuanian public administration, which affects not only the pace of approximation of legislation but also the quality of its implementation and enforcement.

As for the other parts of the *acquis*, Lithuania should not have significant difficulty in applying it from the date of accession in the following fields: education, training and youth; research and technological development; audiovisual; small and medium enterprises; trade and international economic relations; and development.

By contrast, substantial efforts will be needed in the fields of telecommunications; statistics; fisheries; and customs.

Provided that currently positive trends towards industrial restructuring and privatization continue, most of Lithuanian industry should be able to cope with integration within the single market in the medium term.

For the environment, very substantial efforts will be needed, including massive investment and strengthening of administrative capacity to enforce legislation. Full compliance with the *acquis* could only be expected in the long term and would require increased levels of public expenditure.

Lithuania should not have major problems in applying the transport *acquis*, provided that attention is given to maritime safety and environmental standards. Investment will be needed to extend the European transport network so as to ensure that the single market functions well.

It should be possible for Lithuania to achieve the employment and social affairs *acquis* in the medium term, provided that it makes substantial efforts to adapt its legislation to EU requirements in fields such as health and safety and labour law.

On regional policy, Lithuania will need to make the necessary administrative reforms, and establish effective systems of financial control, in order to become able to use the Union's regional and structural funds for its development effectively.

The agriculture sector needs restructuring, and only a limited number of the mechanisms of the common agricultural policy currently exist. A substantial and sustained effort will be required to prepare for accession in the medium term.

In the energy field, Lithuania is heavily dependent on nuclear power generation. It has committed itself to closing the nuclear plant at Ignalina, and must maintain the agreed timetable for this. In the meantime it must make the necessary short-term adjustments to bring safety procedures to internationally accepted standards. No other major problems are foreseen for Lithuanian accession in this sector, though there is a need for further work on monopolies, access to networks and energy pricing.

On the basis of the analysis of Lithuania's capacity to apply the *acquis*, it is not yet possible to be sure when it could become able to take and implement the measures necessary to remove the controls at borders between Lithuania and Member States of the Union.

Lithuania's participation in the third stage of economic and monetary union, which implies coordination of economic policy and complete liberalization of capital movements, still poses problems in the medium term. It is premature to judge whether Lithuania will be in a position, by the time of its accession, to participate in the Euro area. That will depend on how far the success of its structural transformation enables it to achieve and sustain permanently the convergence criteria. These are, however, not a condition for membership.

In justice and home affairs, Lithuania has made some progress, e.g. in the field of asylum. But a significant sustained effort will be needed if it is to be ready to meet the *acquis* in the medium term.

Lithuania should be able to fulfil its obligations in respect of the Common Foreign and Security Policy.

In addition, Lithuania has no major territorial disputes with any Member State or candidate country. It has attached high priority to improving its relations with Poland.

4. *Administrative and Legal Capacity*

For Lithuania to have in the medium term the administrative structures necessary for the essential work of applying and enforcing the *acquis* effectively, there will need to be a major, reinforced effort of reform.

It is not yet possible to judge when Lithuania's judicial system, which has an equally important role to play, will acquire the capacity to play it effectively.

Conclusion

In the light of these considerations, the Commission concludes that:

- Lithuania presents the characteristics of a democracy, with stable institutions guaranteeing the rule of law, human rights and respect for and protection of minorities;
- Lithuania has made considerable progress in the creation of a market economy, but it would face serious difficulties in coping with competitive pressure and market forces within the Union in the medium term;
- Lithuania has made some progress in transposing and implementing the *acquis* relating particularly to the single market. With considerable further effort it should become able to participate fully in the single market in the medium term. Particular efforts, including investment, will be needed to apply the *acquis* fully in sectors such as agriculture, energy and environment. Strengthening of the administrative structure is indispensable if Lithuania is to have the structures to apply and enforce the *acquis* effectively.

In the light of these considerations, the Commission considers that negotiations for accession to the European Union should be opened with Lithuania as soon as it has made sufficient progress in satisfying the conditions of membership defined by the European Council in Copen-hagen.

The reinforced preaccession strategy will help Lithuania to prepare itself better to meet the obligations of membership, and to take action to improve the shortcomings identified in this Opinion. The Commission will present a report no later than the end of 1998 on the progress Lithuania has achieved.

Bulgaria

1. *Political Criteria*

Bulgaria has democratic institutions whose stability seems now secure. They need to be reinforced by fuller respect in practice for the rule of law, at all levels of public administration. Elections are free and fair and led to alternation of power in 1994 and 1997.

Some gaps remain in respect for fundamental rights, though the new government elected in April 1997 has announced a series of positive reforms. Considerable efforts are needed to pursue the fight against cor-ruption, to improve the operation of the judicial system and to protect individual liberties in the face of too frequent abuses by the police and secret services.

The Turkish minority seems well integrated, but this is not so for the Roma.

The current improvement following the arrival in power of a new government permits the conclusion that Bulgaria is on the way to satisfying the political criteria set by the Copenhagen European Council.

2. *Economic Criteria*

Despite some first steps taken in 1991, Bulgaria is still only at the start of the process of structural transformation. The new government has clearly undertaken to the IMF, the World Bank, and the European Commission, that it will set in train rapid reforms in order to free prices and start privatization. This policy should permit recovery from the situ-ation created by the crisis of recent months which saw a negative growth (−10.9 per cent of GDP in 1996), worsening public deficits, hyper-inflation (311 per cent in 1996) and depreciation of the currency.

Bulgaria has a population of 8.3 million and its GDP per capita is 24 per cent of the EU average. The agricultural sector employs more than 20 per cent of the working population and provides 13 per cent of the gross value added. It still has severe structural difficulties despite recent privatization. Trade with the EU has grown significantly and now repre-sents 35 per cent of Bulgaria's external trade.

On the basis of its analysis, the Commission's judgment as to Bul-garia's ability to meet the economic criteria established at Copenhagen is as follows:

Bulgaria's progress in the creation of a market economy has been limited by the absence of a commitment to market-oriented economic policies. Early liberalization of trade and prices was partially reversed, and price controls were not removed until this year. It is only since the crisis at the end of last year, and the recent change of government that consensus about the desirability of economic reforms has begun to develop.

Bulgaria will not be able to cope with competitive pressure and market forces within the Union in the medium term. If the authorities can translate their renewed commitment to economic transition into successful and sustained action, a turnaround in Bulgaria's prospects is possible. However, the country has been set back by six largely wasted years. Incomplete land reform has hampered the emergence of a modern agricultural sector; slow privatization and economic instability have weakened state enterprises and delayed the development of a dynamic private sector.

3. *Capacity to Take on the Obligations of Membership*

Bulgaria has made considerable efforts to meet its obligations under the Europe Agreement. The Agreement has been implemented without major problems and according to the timetable for implementation set out in it. Most of the problems related to implementation have been resolved. But the weakness of the national coordination mechanisms have prevented full exploitation of its potential. The new government has decided to reinforce these structures. Bulgaria has an unsatisfactorily low rate of transposition of the rules and the directives set out in the White Paper.

Bulgarian legislation only incorporates a small part of the *acquis* for the fundamental elements of the single market, except for certain aspects of free circulation of goods. The scale of progress to be achieved requires very substantial and sustained efforts both in approximation of legislation and in creation of structures enabling it to be implemented. Complete restructuring of the financial sector, in order to re-establish public and investor confidence in it, is among the highest priorities, and the government recognizes this.

The weakness of public administration is a major problem, putting in question both the rate and the quality of approximation of legislation. The various structures needed to apply the legislation on the single market are not currently capable of playing their roles.

As for the other parts of the *acquis* Bulgaria should not have particular difficulty in applying the *acquis* in the medium term, provided it maintains its current transposition and modernization efforts, in the following sectors: education, training and youth; research and technological development; fisheries; small and medium enterprises; international trade relations; and development.

By contrast Bulgaria will need to make substantial efforts in order to apply the *acquis* in the fields of telecommunications (particularly price structures), audiovisual, taxation, statistics, consumer protection and customs.

Integration into the European market could pose serious difficulties for Bulgarian industry in the medium term. Many sectors still face important restructuring and privatization needs.

For the environment, very important efforts will be needed including massive investment and strengthening of administrative capacity to enforce legislation. Full compliance with the *acquis* could be expected only in the very long term and would require increased levels of public expenditure.

Bulgaria has made some progress in meeting the transport *acquis*, but serious recent difficulties have held this process back. It must accelerate its efforts in particular in the maritime, air and road freight sectors. Bulgaria must also provide the investment necessary for extending the European transport network, which is an essential element for the effective operation of the single market.

Bulgaria still needs to make substantial efforts to align its procedures in employment and social affairs with EU standards. Progress is needed in particular on labour law and the structure of the labour inspectorate, since these have neither formal autonomy nor the necessary means to fulfil their role properly.

For regional policy, Bulgaria will have to achieve significant preparatory steps, in particular on financial control and the coordination of the different actors involved in policy in this field, before it can effectively use structural funds.

Bulgaria must put in place fundamental reforms of its agricultural sector before it can meet the obligations of accession. Considerable progress is needed on restructuring of the sector; on the agrifood industry; on agricultural policies and on health and quality controls. A particular effort will be needed on the administrative structures responsible for administering the CAP.

For energy, increased efforts must be achieved to prepare for accession, in particular on monopoly operations, price-fixing and state intervention in the solid fuel sector. Bulgaria has a nuclear power station at Kozloduy, which produces around 40 per cent of the country's electricity. It must in the medium term modernize the units for which this is possible, so that they meet internationally accepted standards; and keep its undertaking to close those which cannot be modernized according to the conditions set in the 1993 Agreement. Bulgaria must make a number of modifications to its legislation to comply with Community rules in the nuclear sector and to respect international regimes.

On the basis of the analysis of its capacity to apply the *acquis*, it is not yet possible to be sure when Bulgaria could become able to take and implement the measures necessary to remove the controls at borders between Bulgaria and Member States of the Union.

Bulgarian participation in the third stage of economic and monetary union, which implies coordination of economic policy and complete liberalization of capital movements, poses serious problems in current circumstances, given the substantial structural reforms which still need to be achieved. It is premature to judge whether Bulgaria will be in a position, by the time of its accession, to participate in the Euro area. That will depend on how far the success of its structural transformation enables it to achieve and sustain permanently the convergence criteria. These are, however, not a condition for membership.

Bulgaria faces a particular challenge in justice and home affairs, given the serious difficulties which it faces in these sectors. Only by considerably improving the efficiency of the institutions responsible for action in these fields will Bulgaria become able to apply the *acquis*.

Bulgaria should be able to fulfil its obligations under the Common Foreign and Security Policy.

It has considerably improved its relations with its neighbours and settled almost all its disputes with them.

4. *Administrative and Legal Capacity*

Bulgaria's administrative structures will need a major and sustained effort of reform if it is to become able to apply the *acquis* effectively.

The capacity of the judicial system to ensure uniform application of Community law is of importance for achieving the single market. It is difficult in current circumstances to judge Bulgaria's prospects in this sector.

Conclusion

In the light of these considerations, the Commission concludes that:

- the current improvement in Bulgaria, following the arrival in power of a new government, indicates that Bulgaria is on its way to satisfy the political criteria;
- Bulgaria's progress in the creation of a market economy has been limited by the absence of a commitment to market-oriented economic policies; it would not be able to cope with competitive pressure and market forces within the Union in the medium term;
- despite the progress that has been made, Bulgaria has neither transposed nor taken on the essential elements of the *acquis*, particularly as regards the internal market.

It is therefore uncertain whether Bulgaria will be in a position to assume the obligations of membership in the medium term. In addition, considerable efforts will be needed in the areas of environment, transport, energy, justice and home affairs as well as agriculture. More generally, substantial administrative reform will be indispensable if Bulgaria is to have the structures to apply and enforce the *acquis* effectively.

In the light of these considerations, the Commission considers that negotiations for accession to the European Union should be opened with Bulgaria as soon as it has made sufficient progress in satisfying the conditions of membership defined by the European Council in Copenhagen.

The reinforced preaccession strategy will help Bulgaria to prepare itself better to meet the obligations of membership, and to take action to improve the shortcomings identified in the Opinions. The Commission will present a report no later than the end of 1998 on the progress Bulgaria has achieved.

Czech Republic

1. *Political Criteria*

The Czech Republic's political institutions function properly and in conditions of stability. They respect the limits on their competences and cooperate with each other. Legislative elections in 1992 and 1996 were free and fair. The opposition plays a normal part in the operation of the institutions. Efforts to improve the operation of the judiciary and to intensify the fight against corruption must be sustained.

There are no major problems over respect for fundamental rights. There are, however, some weaknesses in laws governing freedom of the press. Particular attention will need to be paid to the conditions governing any further extension of a law excluding from public service members of the former security services and active members of the communist regime. There is a problem of discrimination affecting the Roma, notably through the operation of the citizenship law.

The Czech Republic presents the characteristics of a democracy, with stable institutions guaranteeing the rule of law, human rights, and respect for and protection of minorities.

2. *Economic Criteria*

After some disruption caused by the separation of the Czech and Slovak Republics in 1993, economic growth resumed in 1994 and has been strongly sustained since, though at a lower rate (4.0 per cent) in 1996. The Czech Republic has maintained tight fiscal policies, but both trade and current account deficits grew in 1996. Inflation has gradually declined over recent years, and stood at 8.8 per cent in 1996. GDP per head is about 55 per cent of the EU average, for a population of 10.3 million. The agricultural sector employed 6 per cent of the labour force in 1995, and accounted for 5 per cent of gross value added. The EU's share of Czech trade has risen from 27 per cent in 1989 (as Czechoslovakia) to 55 per cent.

On the basis of its analysis, the Commission's judgment as to the Czech Republic's ability to meet the economic criteria established at Copenhagen is as follows:

The Czech Republic can be regarded as a functioning market economy. Market mechanisms operate widely, and the role of the state in the economy has been completely changed. Substantial success has been achieved in stabilizing the economy. Unemployment is among the lowest in Europe. However, as the recent emergence of macroeconomic imbalances has shown, further progress will need to be made over the next few years, notably in strengthening corporate governance and the financial system.

The Czech Republic should be able to cope with competitive pressure and market forces within the Union in the medium term, provided that change at the enterprise level is accelerated. The country benefits from a trained and skilled workforce, and infrastructure is relatively good. Investment in the economy has been high in recent years, with foreign direct investment also strong. The country has successfully reoriented its trade towards the west. But although the quality of exported goods is improving, their value added is still low. The banking sector is dominated by a few, partly state-owned banks and its competitive position is not strong. The main challenge for the Czech Republic is to press on with enterprise restructuring in order to improve the medium term performance of the economy and as a way of redressing the imbalances on the external side.

3. *Capacity to Take on the Obligations of Membership*

The Czech Republic has already adopted significant elements of the provisions of the Europe Agreement, and according to the timetable for implementation set out in it. Few serious bilateral problems have arisen, though the Czech imposition in April 1997 of an import deposit scheme was not in conformity with the Agreement. The Czech Republic has achieved a satisfactory rate of transposition of the rules and directives identified in the White Paper, though there is still a considerable amount of legislative work left to do.

For most of the areas relating specifically to the single market, the legislative basis is more or less in place. In certain fields, particularly financial services and taxation, further work is still needed.

Notwithstanding the efforts which have been made, the real progress made in transposing legislation still needs to be accompanied by concrete measures of implementation, as well as establishment of an effective administrative underpinning. Overall, the administrative infrastructure is either well established or recently set up and functioning normally. But substantial further efforts are needed.

As for the other parts of the *acquis*, the Czech Republic should not have difficulty in applying it from the date of accession in the following fields: education, training and youth; research and technological development; telecommunications; statistics; consumer protection; small and medium enterprises; trade and international economic relations; and development.

By contrast, substantial efforts will be needed for the Czech Republic to be able to apply the *acquis* in the fields of audiovisual, and customs (though efforts are under way in this sector).

Provided that past and current efforts at industrial restructuring and modernization are continued, and reinforced in the case of heavy industries, most sectors of Czech industry should face no major problems in integrating into the single market in the medium term.

For the environment, very substantial efforts will be needed, including massive investment and strengthening of administrative capacity to enforce legislation. Partial compliance with the *acquis* could be achieved in the medium term. Full compliance could be achieved only in the long term.

For transport, the Czech government has already made notable progress towards meeting the *acquis*. Efforts need to be pursued in respect of road freight transport. But meeting the *acquis* relating to the single market should not pose real problems. Investment will be needed to extend the European transport network so as to ensure that the single market functions well.

In order to apply the employment and social affairs *acquis* in the medium term, work is needed to adapt legislation in the field of health and safety at work.

In the field of regional policy and cohesion, if the Czech Republic works to establish the necessary administrative framework and achieve the substantial improvement needed in the field of financial control, it should be able in the medium term to use the Union's regional and structural funds for its development effectively.

For agriculture, particular efforts will be needed to implement veterinary and phytosanitary requirements and to strengthen the administrative structures necessary to apply the common agricultural policy instruments. Provided these targets can be met, accession in the medium term should not be accompanied by significant problems in applying the common agricultural policy in an appropriate manner.

On energy, the Czech Republic has a substantial nuclear power programme, which is due to expand further. The modernization programme needed to bring the nuclear plants at Dukovny and Temelin up to internationally accepted safety standards must be completed within 7–10 years. The Czech Republic should be able to comply with the rest of the *acquis* in the medium term, given further work on energy pricing, state intervention in the solid fuel sector and access to networks.

On the basis of the analysis of its capacity to apply the *acquis*, the Czech Republic could be in a position in the medium term to take and implement the measures necessary for removal of controls at its borders with Member States of the Union. If part of its current borders became part of the Union's external border, reinforcement of border controls would be needed.

The Czech Republic's participation in the third stage of economic and monetary union, which implies coordination of economic policy and complete liberalization of capital movements, should pose no problems in the medium term. But it is premature to judge whether the Czech Republic will be in a position, by the time of its accession, to participate in the Euro area. That will depend on how far the success of its structural transformation enables it to achieve and sustain permanently the convergence criteria. These are, however, not a condition for membership.

The Czech Republic is likely to comply with the justice and home affairs *acquis* in the next few years, provided that existing progress is maintained, including in the fight against drugs and organized crime.

The Czech Republic should be able to fulfil its obligations in respect of the Common Foreign and Security Policy.

In addition, the Czech Republic has no territorial disputes with any Member State or neighbouring candidate country. All its state frontiers are regulated by Treaty. There remain some minor issues in its relationship with Slovakia.

4. *Administrative and Legal Capacity*

For the Czech Republic to have in the medium term the administrative structures necessary for the essential work of applying and enforcing the *acquis* effectively, there will need to be a significant and sustained effort of reform.

It is not yet possible to judge when the Czech Republic's judicial system, which has an equally important role to play, will acquire the capacity to play it effectively, though reform will clearly be required.

Conclusion

In the light of these considerations, the Commission concludes that:

- the Czech Republic presents the characteristics of a democracy, with stable institutions guaranteeing the rule of law, human rights and respect for and protection of minorities;
- the Czech Republic can be regarded as a functioning market economy, and it should be able to cope with competitive pressure and market forces within the Union in the medium term;

- if the Czech Republic continues its efforts on transposition of the *acquis* relating to the single market, and intensifies work on its implementation, the Czech Republic should become capable in the medium term of applying it fully. The import deposit scheme will need to be resolved within the terms of the Europe Agreement. Particular effort, including investment, will be needed to meet the *acquis* in sectors such as agriculture, environment and energy. Further administrative reform will be indispensable if the Czech Republic is to have the structures to apply and enforce the *acquis* fully.

In the light of these considerations, the Commission recommends that negotiations for accession should be opened with Czech Republic.

The reinforced preaccession strategy will help the Czech Republic to prepare itself better to meet the obligations of membership, and to take action to improve the shortcomings identified in this Opinion. The Commission will present a report no later than the end of 1998 on the progress it has achieved.

Slovenia

1. *Political Criteria*

The Slovene institutions function properly, with the different powers respecting the limits on their competencies and cooperating with each other. Elections in 1992 and 1996 were free and fair. The opposition plays a normal part in the operation of the institutions.

There are no major problems over respect for fundamental rights. Some improvements are still needed in the operation of the judicial system, and in restoring property to former owners dispossessed under the communist regime. The effectiveness of the fight against corruption needs further strengthening.

Slovenia therefore presents the characteristics of a democracy with stable institutions guaranteeing the rule of law, human rights and respect for and protection of minorities.

2. *Economic Criteria*

After a period of falling GDP, Slovenia has had positive growth since 1993 (5.3 per cent in 1994, 3.9 per cent in 1995, 3.1 per cent in 1996). This has been achieved in conditions of balance in public finances and external accounts, and falling inflation (9.1 per cent in 1996). Slovenia has 2 million inhabitants and GDP per capita is 59 per cent of the EU average. The agricultural sector employs nearly 7 per cent of the working population and contributes 5 per cent of gross value added. Trade relations with the EU have grown considerably since 1991 and now represent 65 per cent of Slovenia's external trade.

On the basis of its analysis, the Commission's judgment as to Slovenia's ability to meet the economic criteria established at Copenhagen is as follows:

Slovenia can be regarded as a functioning market economy. It has advanced considerably in liberalization and privatization, and achieved a successful stabilization of the economy. However, there is a lack of competition in some sectors, in particular the financial sector, the working of the market mechanisms still needs some improvement and the necessary reforms of the fiscal and social security systems are not yet completed.

Slovenia should be able to cope with competitive pressure and market forces within the Union in the medium term, provided that rigidities in the economy are reduced. It has a diverse export base, the workforce is skilled and highly trained, and infrastructure is relatively good. However, enterprise restructuring has been slow due to the consensual character of economic decision-making, and the incentives of workers and managers to preserve the status quo. Improvements in competitiveness have been hampered by rapid wage growth combined with low productivity growth. The low level of foreign direct investment reflects these structural problems, which need to be tackled.

3. *Capacity to Take on the Obligations of Membership*

Slovenia, which has not yet ratified the Europe Agreement, has made some progress in applying the corresponding dispositions of the Interim Agreement, and has achieved a satisfactory rate of transposition of the rules and directives set out in the White Paper.

For most of the sectors related to the single market, and in particular on accounting, mutual recognition of professional qualifications and intellectual property, the legislative foundation is virtually in place. According to the Slovene authorities' own estimation, most of the necessary measures have been either partly or completely transposed. But further legislative effort will be needed to achieve full absorption of the *acquis*.

Notwithstanding the efforts which have been made, the progress made in transposing legislation still needs to be accompanied by concrete measures of implementation, as well as by the establishment of an effective administrative underpinning. Substantial work is still needed in the fields of public procurement, competition, insurance, freedom of capital movements, product conformity and standardization. Introduction of VAT is a top priority. Implementation and application of legislation should be seen as essential elements of Slovenia's preaccession strategy. Slovenia needs to go beyond primary legislation and cover also technical standards.

As for the other parts of the *acquis*, if it continues its efforts, Slovenia should not have particular difficulties in applying it in the medium term in the following fields: education, training and youth; research and technical development; telecommunications; audiovisual; small and medium enterprises; consumer protection; international trade relations; development; and customs.

The current level and perspective for competitiveness of most of the Slovene industry enables a positive expectation of its capacity to cope with the competitive pressure and market forces within the Union in the medium term. There may, however, be problems linked to certain labour market rigidities and for those sectors and companies which have not yet undergone restructuring.

For the environment, very important efforts will be needed, including massive investment and strengthening of administrative capacity for enforcement of legislation. Full compliance with the *acquis* could only be expected in the long term and would necessitate increased levels of public expenditure.

Slovenia has already made satisfactory progress in the transport field. If it continues its efforts in road freight transport and the railway sector, transport should not pose difficulties for accession. Slovenia has undertaken to make the investments necessary to establish TENs in order to ensure effective functioning of the single market.

Slovenia should also be able to apply the *acquis* on employment and social affairs in the medium term. Efforts are still needed, however, on labour law and health and safety at work. Slovenia also needs to establish the autonomy of the labour inspectorate.

As for regional policy and cohesion Slovenia has adopted a development policy which should permit it in the medium term to implement Community rules and effectively use structural funds. But it will need to strengthen considerably its financial control mechanisms.

In agriculture, if progress is achieved on veterinary and phytosanitary controls, on strengthening the structures needed to apply the CAP, and on restructuring the agrifood sector as well as on strengthening its rural development policy, membership should not create significant problems for Slovenia in the medium term in applying the CAP in an appropriate manner.

In energy efforts are still needed on monopoly operations, price fixing, access to networks and state intervention in the solid fuel sector. Slovenia has a nuclear power station at Krsko, which it shares with Croatia, and which produces 20 per cent of its electricity. It was built according to western technology. A solution needs to be found for its nuclear waste.

On the basis of the analysis of its capacity to apply the *acquis*, Slovenia could be in a position in the medium term to take and implement the measures necessary for removal of controls at its borders with Member States of the Union.

Slovenia's participation in the third stage of economic and monetary union, which implies coordination of economic policy and the complete liberalization of capital movements, could present some difficulties given the incompatibility of the rules governing the central bank with those of the EU, and also the need to restructure the banking sector. It is premature to judge whether Slovenia will be in a position, by the time of its accession, to participate in the Euro area. That will depend on how far the success of its structural transformation enables it to achieve and sustain permanently the convergence criteria. These are, however, not a condition for membership.

Slovenia should be able to apply the *acquis* on justice and home affairs in the next few years, even if particular attention needs to be paid to the operation of the judicial system, treatment of asylum seekers and the fight against organized crime.

Slovenia should be able to fulfil its obligations in respect of the Common Foreign and Security Policy.

Since 1991 Slovenia has strengthened its relations with its neighbours and signed Friendship and Good Neighbourliness Treaties with them. There is, however, still a dispute with Croatia over maritime boundaries.

4. Administrative and Legal Capacity

If Slovenia undertakes substantial efforts to reform its administration, the necessary structures could be in place in the medium term to apply the *acquis* effectively.

The capacity of the judicial system to ensure correct and uniform application of Community law is important, particularly for achievement of the single market. In current circumstances it is difficult to judge Slovenia's progress in this field.

Conclusion

In the light of these considerations, the Commission concludes that:

- Slovenia presents the characteristics of a democracy, with stable institutions guaranteeing the rule of law, human rights and respect for and protection of minorities;
- Slovenia can be regarded as a functioning market economy and should be able to cope with competitive pressure and market forces within the Union in the medium term;
- Slovenia has to make considerable efforts to take on the *acquis*, particularly as regards the effective application in the area of the internal market. In addition, important progress will be necessary in the sector of environment, employment and social affairs and energy. More generally, further administrative reform will be indispensable if Slovenia is to have the structures to apply and enforce the *acquis* effectively.

In the light of these considerations, the Commission recommends that negotiations for accession should be opened with Slovenia.

The reinforced preaccession strategy will help Slovenia to prepare itself better to meet the obligations of membership, and to take action to improve the shortcomings identified in the Opinions. The Commission will present a report no later than the end of 1998 on the progress Slovenia has achieved.

5|

The Mediterranean Dimension

The next enlargement of the EU is often described as the 'eastern enlargement' but it is important not to forget the southern dimension. Ever since the EU and Turkey signed an association agreement in 1963, Turkey has pursued its ambition of full EU membership making a formal application for membership to the Council of Ministers in April 1987. The EU ambitions of Cyprus and Malta developed at a later stage, and it was in July 1990 that they applied for membership.

Turkey

Turkey's application for membership resulted in the presentation of the Commission's Opinion on 20 December 1989. The Commission concluded that 'it would be inappropriate for the Community—which is itself undergoing major changes while the whole of Europe is in a state of flux—to become involved in a new accession negotiation at this stage. Furthermore, the political and economic situation in Turkey leads the Commission to believe that it would not be useful to open accession negotiations with Turkey straight away.'

The Commission went on to argue, however, that

> the Community has a fundamental interest in intensifying its relations with Turkey and helping it to complete as soon as possible its process of political and economic modernization. To contribute to the success of Turkey's modernization efforts, the Commission recommends that the Community propose to Turkey a series of substantial measures which, without casting doubt on its eligibility for membership of the Community, would enable both partners to enter now on the road towards increased interdependence and integration, in accordance with the political will shown at the time of the signing of the Ankara Treaty. These measures will focus on the following four aspects corresponding to Turkey's aspirations and needs: completion of the customs union, the resumption and intensification of financial cooperation, the promotion of

industrial and technological cooperation, and the strengthening of political and cultural links. These measures should be situated in the framework of the Association Agreement which currently governs relations between Turkey and the Community.[1]

The Commission's position on Turkey was largely shared by Member States but attempts to strengthen relations with Turkey were often handicapped by the poor relations between Greece and Turkey.

An important milestone in the development of the EU's relations with Turkey came with the signature of the Customs Union agreement which entered into force on 31 December 1995. The Customs Union brought a new intensity to EU–Turkish relations even if its full implementation, especially the financial assistance package, was delayed due to continuing Greek–Turkish disputes over Cyprus and the Aegean.

In April 1997 a meeting of the Association Council reaffirmed Turkish eligibility and confirmed that Turkey would be judged by the same objective standards and criteria as other applicants and a Commission communication of 16 July 1997, published to coincide with Agenda 2000, sketched out proposals to further deepen cooperation.

In the Communication, the Commission considered

> that the Association Council's confirmation of Turkey's eligibility for EU membership and its statement that Turkey will be judged by the same objective standards and criteria as other applicants have given a new impetus to EU–Turkey relations. Further strengthening of EU–Turkey relations will depend on progress by Turkey in a number of fields. In the political field, democratization needs to be further pursued. There should be an improvement of relations between Greece and Turkey; respect for the principles of international law; and an effective programme to bring Turkish human rights standards up to internationally accepted levels. Human rights and the rule of law need to be respected, especially in the context of the fight against terrorism and the search for a non-military solution to the problem Turkey is facing in the south-east, which is still under a state of emergency. Moreover, Turkey should contribute actively to a just and lasting settlement of the Cyprus question in accordance with the relevant UN resolutions. Despite the remarkable dynamism of the Turkish private sector, there is a need for economic reform and a policy of stable public finances, prices and monetary policy to promote sustainable economic and employment growth. Continuing reform of the state sector and of agriculture is needed and the adaptation of the physical and social infrastructure of the country poses major financial and administrative challenges. In parallel with improvements in

1.   sec(89)2290, 20 December 1989.

these areas, the initiatives suggested above can enable the EU and Turkey to achieve a higher degree of integration, to the benefit of all their citizens, by further developing the links established by the Association Agreement and the custom union. This will bring greater stability, security and prosperity to the EU and Turkey and assist Turkey in realizing its European vocation.[2]

There is no doubt that Turkey is a country of major strategic importance for the EU (and for NATO). As a long-standing aspirant for EU membership, Turkish frustrations at being overtaken by some Central and Eastern European states, not to mention Cyprus, is understandable. But the criteria for EU accession have to be applied uniformly and objectively. Even in the medium term, there are likely to remain significant obstacles to Turkey's fulfilling the criteria for EU membership. It is imperative, therefore, that EU–Turkish relations develop on a sound and realistic footing and every opportunity be sought to deepen the relationship. One such opportunity may be the European Conference, the proposal put forward by the Commission in Agenda 2000 to bring together Member States and candidate countries to discuss issues of common concern.

Cyprus

In June 1993 the Commission published its Opinion on the Cypriot application for membership. The Commission stated that:

it was convinced that the result of Cyprus's accession to the Community will be increased security and prosperity and that it would help bring the two communities on the island closer together. If there were to be a political settlement, the prospect of the progressive re-establishment of fundamental liberties would help overcome the inevitable practical difficulties which would arise during the transition period in regard to the adoption of the relevant Community legislation. In regard to economic aspects, in view of the progress towards a customs union achieved thus far, the adoption of the *acquis communautaire* by Cyprus will pose no insurmountable problems. The Commission is not underestimating the problems that the economic transition poses. However, the economy of the southern part of the island has demonstrated an ability to adapt and seems ready to face the challenge of integration provided that the work already started on reforms and on opening up to the outside world is maintained, notably in the context of the customs union. This Opinion has also shown that there will be a greater chance of narrowing the

2.   COM(97) 394 of 16 July 1997.

development gap between north and south in the event of Cyprus's integration with the Community.

Turning to the wider issues of the Cyprus question, the Commission continued:

> Even though they object to the conditions under which the application for membership was made, the leaders of the Turkish-Cypriot community are fully conscious of the economic and social benefits that integration with Europe would bring their community. This opinion has also shown that Cyprus's integration with the Community implies a peaceful, balanced and lasting settlement of the Cyprus question—a settlement which will make it possible for the two communities to be reconciled, for confidence to be re-established and for their respective leaders to work together. While safeguarding the essential balance between the two communities and the right of each to preserve its fundamental interests, the institutional provisions contained in such a settlement should create the appropriate conditions for Cyprus to participate normally in the decision-making process of the European Community and in the correct application of Community law throughout the island. In view of all the above and in the expectation of significant progress in the talks currently being pursued under the auspices of the Secretary-General of the United Nations, the Commission feels that a positive signal should be sent to the authorities and the people of Cyprus as eligible for membership and that as soon as the prospect of a settlement is surer, the Community is ready to start the process with Cyprus that should eventually lead to its accession.[3]

In June 1994 the European Council agreed that Cyprus (and Malta) should be involved in the next enlargement and that negotiations should begin six months after the conclusion of the Intergovernmental Conference (IGC) due to commence in 1996.

In its 1993 opinion the Commission noted the Republic of Cyprus's advanced level of development and economic dynamism. This still holds good with full employment (2.5 per cent jobless rate), moderate inflation (3 per cent) and public debt standing at 53 per cent of GNP in 1996. The southern part of the island should not encounter any major problems in adopting the *acquis communautaire* or in coping with competition inside the EU. However, there is a need to align regulations and practices in the financial sector more fully with those which apply in the Union and to reinforce cooperation and controls in all areas of justice and home affairs.

3.   COM (93) 313 of 31 July 1993.

In northern Cyprus the trends observed by the Commission in 1993 remain unchanged. Average income per capita is about ECU 3600 per annum, one-third of that of the southern part of the island. The economy is becoming increasingly dependent on the public sector, which ultimately means financial transfers from Turkey. Investments remain low despite its human and natural resources.

The 1993 Opinion noted the continuing division of Cyprus. Efforts since then, chiefly under UN auspices, to work towards a political settlement, in accordance with various UN proposals, have not achieved much progress. The UN conducted intensive contacts with the leaders of the two communities during the first half of 1997 which have now led to face-to-face talks between them under UN auspices. The shape of a settlement, establishing a bicommunal and bizonal federation, is well established, and supported by the Union. A number of options for constitutional and territorial arrangements to implement it have been explored, and the beginnings of a possible consensus have sometimes been discernible. But there has not hitherto been sufficient incentive for the two communities to reach agreement.

The Union is determined to play a positive role in bringing about a just and lasting settlement in accordance with the relevant United Nations resolutions. The status quo, which is at odds with international law, threatens the stability of the island and the region and has implications for the security of Europe as a whole. The Union has made clear that it cannot, and does not wish to, interfere in the institutional arrangements to be agreed between the parties. But it is available to advise on the compatibility of such arrangements with the *acquis* of the Union. The prospect of accession, whose political and economic advantages are now becoming clear to Turkish Cypriots as well as to Greek Cypriots, can in itself provide such an incentive.

The timetable agreed for accession negotiations to start with Cyprus means that they could start before a political settlement is reached. The Union shares the view expressed by the UN Secretary-General, that the decision to open negotiations should be seen as a positive development which could promote the search for a political settlement.

Negotiations on accession would be facilitated if sufficient progress were to be made between the parties in contacts during 1998 under the auspices of the United Nations to allow representatives of the Turkish Cypriot community to be involved in the accession process. Agreement on a political settlement would permit a faster conclusion to the negotiations. If progress towards a settlement is not made before the negotiations are due to begin, they should be opened with the government of the Republic of Cyprus, as the only authority recognized by international law.

The division of the island since the Turkish intervention in 1974 raises several problems in the context of enlargement. How could a divided island implement the internal market? How would the enlargement process be seen by Turkey? How would problems over Cyprus affect the pace of eastward enlargement? The Union hopes that the prospect of accession will provide a catalyst to bring about a just and lasting settlement. If this is achieved, it will greatly promote stability in the region, particularly with regard to Greek–Turkish relations, as well as EU–Turkish relations.

Malta

The Commission's Opinion on Malta was published in June 1993 simultaneously with that of Cyprus. It affirmed that

> Malta's culture and history, reflecting the deep links with several of the peoples of Europe, have for centuries developed a European identity.' Bearing in mind the country's democratic status and its consistent respect for human rights, Malta is entirely justified in asserting its vocation for membership of the European Union; a right that should be confirmed by the Community.
>
> However, in so doing, the Community must also satisfy itself that Malta's application is such as to hold out every chance of a satisfactory conclusion of the accession negotiations, followed by successful integration into the Community and the European Union. This Opinion has put forward a series of assessments, queries and proposals with regard to the more difficult questions raised by Malta's application, namely the need to reform the overall regulatory framework of the Maltese economy, the question of the compatibility of its neutrality and non-alignment with the provisions of the Maastricht Treaty, and the issue of Malta's participation in the European institutions. In the light of these assessments and of Malta's indisputably European calling, the Commission feels that it is important to send to the authorities and people of Malta a positive signal to encourage them to undertake vigorously the requisite reforms to transform Malta's economy into an open and competitive one.
>
> The Commission is convinced that such a signal could be given by announcing that the Community is willing to open accession negotiations with Malta as soon as conditions allow. An announcement along these lines would have the effect of mobilizing public support for the

reform process in Malta. It remains, therefore, for Malta and the Community to start now to lay the foundations for the success of this
strategy.[4]

The Maltese application was not universally supported by the population. The Labour Party were opposed to full membership citing taxation
and employment reasons and following the general election of 26
October 1996, won by the Labour Party, Malta stated that it did not
wish to pursue its membership application. Although Malta has frozen
its application for membership of the Union, enlargement may well
trigger renewed interest in full membership.

Euro-Med

The final phase of eastern enlargement may coincide with the
Barcelona timetable, which envisages a Europe-Med Free Trade Area
(FTA) by 2010. Eastern enlargement and in particular economic competition from the CEECs (including their share of Foreign Direct
Investment [FDI]) could be perceived as a threat to Med–EU trade
relations. The CEECs, because of their proximity, existing product
complementarity, industrial traditions and advanced economic transformation, could make the position of the Med 12[5] more fragile. This
situation could worsen further as a result of the progressive elimination
of trade restrictions by Mediterranean countries.

Given the strategic importance and potential new security risks ema-
nating from the region, it is important that the enlarged Union should
not neglect its relations with the Mediterranean but pursue the policies
agreed at Barcelona with vigour. Indeed there may be scope for new
imaginative thinking about future EU–Mediterranean relations involving enhanced political and economic ties. Suggestions include the
establishment of a Europe-Maghreb (or a Europe-Mediterranean) Bank;
and a more structured relationship between the various technical assistance programmes (Phare/Tacis/Meda)[6] and European Investment Bank

4.   COM (93) 312 of 31 July 1993.
5.   The Med 12 are, in alphabetical order: Algeria, Cyprus, Egypt, Israel,
Jordan, Lebanon, Malta, Morocco, the Palestinian Authority, Syria, Tunisia and
Turkey.
6.   Tacis is the technical assistance programme for the newly independent
states. Meda is the technical assistance programme for the Mediterranean countries
covered in the Barcelona process.

facilities. Although the final outcome will be qualitatively different (membership for the CEECs—Free Trade Area for the Mediterranean 12), EU interests to the east and south will remain broadly similar: political and economic stability; economic convergence and trade integration; promotion of democracy, human rights and good governance; continued economic transformation.

6 |

Agenda 2000

The Opinions covered in Chapter 4 formed part of the Commission's comprehensive package entitled 'Agenda 2000: For a Stronger and Wider Union', submitted to Council and Parliament on 15 July 1997. The package consisted essentially of the Commission's recommendations for the Union's financial framework for the period 2000–2006; the future development of the Union's policies, and in particular its two most important spending policies—the cohesion and structural funds, and the Common Agricultural Policy; and the strategy for enlargement of the Union.

These three basic elements—budgets, policies, enlargement—are closely linked with each other, not simply because the budget is the expression of the financial resources planned for the other two elements, but also because the development of the Union's policies has implications for the process of its enlargement, and vice versa. This package approach, on which the Commission strongly insisted, was widely welcomed in Council and Parliament as a rational and desirable means of ensuring coherence between the different elements; and despite the reservations of Member States on this or that aspect of the package, and the temptation to dissociate some parts from the others, the basic linkages are likely to remain until all the main decisions are taken on Agenda 2000. There will continue to be tensions between the different groups of ministers responsible, meeting in the Council in its different compositions; finance ministers will wish to have the last word on budgets, agriculture ministers on agriculture, regional ministers on structural funds, and everyone will wish to influence the foreign ministers' discussions on enlargement, since the conditions for enlargement will affect almost every area of the Union's policies. But it can be hoped that the package approach, and the ultimate authority of the European Council, will impose order and coherence on the series of decisions to be taken.

The inclusion of three elements in a single package, and the unveiling of the package shortly after the conclusion of the Intergovernmental Conference (IGC) at Amsterdam in June 1997, were not a coincidence. Already in the early stages of preparation for the IGC, which commenced in March 1996, there was a risk of all sorts of different questions being dragged into the intergovernmental debate, and of its agenda being inflated to unmanageable proportions. If the Conference was to discuss everything, including the future development of the budget and of the Union's main policies, it could last for a very long time and ultimately decide nothing. It was for this reason that the European Council in Madrid, already in December 1995 even before the opening of the IGC, effectively took enlargement and the post-1999 budget arrangements out of the orbit of the IGC, by inviting the Commission to submit its Opinions on the applications for membership, together with a 'composite paper' on enlargement as soon as possible after the conclusion of the IGC, and also to submit a communication on the future financial framework, having regard to the prospect of enlargement, immediately after the IGC. This wise strategic decision kept the IGC on track, and sowed the seeds for Agenda 2000.

Within the Commission, the decision was later taken to bring together the budgetary communication and the enlargement documents into a single package, for which the inspired title 'Agenda 2000' was invented—a title which has the advantage not only of brevity and originality, but also of viability in all of the Union's official languages. The 'composite paper' then lost its separate identity, becoming simply a part of the basic document Agenda 2000; and from the linguistic point of view, this was a happy conclusion, since the title 'composite paper' threatened to be one of the least exciting titles ever to emerge from the Commission (in fact, the expression 'composite paper' is believed to have been coined by translators confronted by the French expression *document d'ensemble* in the text of the conclusions of Madrid).

It is worth recalling that the window of opportunity thus presented after the conclusion of the IGC, for the Commission to launch an important initiative, came exactly in the middle of the five-year term of office of the Commission presided by Jacques Santer. The Commission was well disposed, in mid-term, to launch an initiative defining the agenda for important decisions during the rest of its mandate. The precedent of the successful packages launched earlier by the Commission under the presidency of Jacques Delors, widely known as the

'Delors 1 and 2 packages', was also a guiding factor, and Agenda 2000 was sometimes referred to as the 'Santer package', or even 'Jacques 3'.

Because the Agenda 2000 package has been presented and published in a number of different forms, including official summaries and extracts, it is useful to explain its precise articulation and contents. As adopted by the Commission on 15 July 1997, it comprised:

1. 'Agenda 2000: For a Stronger and Wider Union', the basic document COM(97)2000 Vol. I, containing:

   Part One   – The Policies of the Union
   Part Two   – The Challenge of Enlargement
   Part Three – The New Financial Framework (2000–2006)

2. 'Agenda 2000: The Challenge of Enlargement', a supplementary document COM(97)2000 Vol. II comprizing two texts:

   (a) 'Reinforcing the Preaccession Strategy', giving details of the new priorities for Phare, other forms of preaccession aid, the new Accession Partnerships and so on.
   (b) 'The Effects on the Union's Policies of Enlargement to the Applicant Countries of Central and Eastern Europe', known as the Impact Study.

3. Ten 'Commission Opinions on Applications for Membership' from the countries of Central and Eastern Europe, documents COM(97)2001–2010: the numbers and sequence of these documents correspond to the chronological order in which the ten applications were submitted, beginning with Hungary.

The package was distributed, immediately on 16 July, in a printed form consisting of three volumes:

1. 'Agenda 2000: 1. For a Stronger and Wider Union' (Volume I of document COM(97)2000)
2. 'Agenda 2000: 2. The Challenge of Enlargement' (Volume II of the same document)
3. 'Agenda 2000: 3. The Opinions of the European Commission on the Applications for Accession—Summaries and Conclusion' (extracts from the ten Opinions).

Subsequently, in the course of 1997, the documents were published as Supplements to the Bulletin of the European Union:

1. Supplement 5/97 entitled 'Agenda 2000: For a Stronger and Wider Union', comprizing in one volume Agenda 2000, Reinforcing the Pre-accession Strategy, and the Impact Study.
2. Supplements 6/97 to 15/97, comprizing the full texts of the ten Opinions, in separate volumes.

'Agenda 2000' is set against the background of a broadly positive review of European integration stretching from the 1986 Single Act to the Treaty of Amsterdam in June 1997 and embracing the coming challenges from both within and without. It picks out the far-reaching changes that have affected Europe over the last decade (two enlargements, two major reviews of the treaties, two significant financial packages) and stresses the new impetus for integration triggered by these developments as well as by changes in the outside world (particularly the end of the Cold War and the collapse of the Soviet Union).

The very real successes chalked up by the Union over this period should not, however, obscure the difficulties. The current recession has led to an unacceptable level of unemployment and has made Member States' own budget and structural reforms harder to accomplish. On the positive side, these factors have stimulated efforts to achieve more convergence and coordination with a view to economic and monetary union and to turn to account the Union's potential as a single economic entity. Among the political and psychological difficulties, the Commission stresses the perceived distance between the Union and its citizens. The Treaty of Amsterdam will help to narrow this gap by strengthening the idea of a 'citizen's Europe', bolstering the Union's capabilities beyond its borders and reforming its institutions.

Work on the institutional reforms still remains to be completed, however. The Commission proposes that the political decision on the weighting of votes in the Council, which is meant to go hand in hand with a reduction in the number of Members of the Commission by first enlargement, should be taken well before the year 2000. A further IGC should be called as soon as possible after 2000 to prepare the Union for enlargement by means of far-reaching reforms of the institutional provisions in the Treaty, including the generalized introduction of qualified majority voting.

The Commission also outlines certain long-term trends of relevance to the way the Union functions. These include the concerns of the man and woman in the street, population trends, new technologies, restructuring of markets and enterprises, and the globalization of the economy and the emergence of a multipolar world.

The successful passage to EMU and the full exploitation of the potential of the single market will enhance Europe as an economic entity, contributing to sustainable growth. Its competitiveness depends on dynamic enterprises and the skills and knowledge of its people. In order to turn growth into jobs, employment systems should be modernized. Beyond these economic goals, Europeans also want a cohesive and inclusive society based on solidarity, as well as a high quality of life, sound environment, freedom, security and justice. The internal policies of the Union should be more resolutely oriented towards meeting these objectives.

The priority policy goal of economic and social cohesion must be steadfastly adhered to. Indeed, the prospect of enlargement encompassing new countries with widely diverging levels of development makes this even more necessary than before. European-wide solidarity will be needed more than ever if we are to achieve the major objective of reducing disparities in development, as set out explicitly in Article 130a of the Treaty. Cohesion policy is an essential contribution towards stability in the Union and promoting a high level of employment. Constant efforts must be made to tackle the regions' uneven capabilities for generating sustainable development and their difficulties in adapting to new conditions on the labour market, which call for greater capacity to foresee and prepare for the skills both men and women will need in future. Assistance from the structural funds must foster competitive development and lasting growth to create jobs throughout the Union.

The 1992 reform of the Common Agricultural Policy has been highly successful. But the time has come to deepen the reform and to take further the movement towards world market prices coupled to direct income aids. Several reasons militate in favour of such an approach: the risk of new market imbalances, the prospect of a new trade round, the aspiration towards a more environment-friendly and quality-oriented agriculture, and last but not least the perspective of enlargement. At the same time, there is a growing need for a fully fledged rural development policy.

In its external relations, the time has come for the Union to develop a fully operational foreign policy. The Amsterdam Treaty gives it more adequate instruments to develop its Common Foreign and Security Policy. The single currency provides it with a unique opportunity to become a leading financial player. Enlargement will enhance its influence. There is a genuine call for an identifiable Europe, whose partnership and cooperation is being sought after worldwide.

The Union must respond positively, both because it has political and economic interests to defend and because it has a major contribution to bring to peace, democracy and the defence of human rights and values.

The Union's internal and external environment is undergoing rapid change. Even more than in the past, it must focus on what is essential and give priority to areas where it can provide real added value. In this connection, by virtue of its right of initiative, the Commission's role is of crucial importance in steering Union policies in new directions. At the same time, the Commission must rethink its work and improve its management, coordination and monitoring capacities. In a wider and more diverse Europe, its role as defender of the Community interest will be even more decisive than in the past. To succeed, it must reorganize and modernize.

The new financial framework put forward by the Commission is designed to enable the Union to finance its essential requirements over the medium term: the cost of continuing to reform the Common Agricultural Policy, pursuing the priority goal of economic and social cohesion, strengthening internal policies in fields where Community action can contribute towards growth and employment, enhancing the preaccession aid to applicant countries and absorbing the impact of the first enlargement.

The Commission considers that these challenges can be met in budget terms within the ceiling on own resources that will be reached in 1999 that is 1.27 per cent of the Union's GNP.

The Commission notes that the financing system has been operating adequately and it foresees no changes in the budget positions of the Member States which would be so far-reaching as to demand a revision of the financing mechanism laid down in the 'own-resources' decision of 31 October 1994. A fundamental review of own resources should be embarked upon once the Union is faced with raising the present ceiling. If major changes then appear in the budget positions of the Member States, the introduction of a generalized corrective mechanism, including the British correction, could then be considered.

The chapters of 'Agenda 2000' on the challenge posed by enlargement form the 'composite paper' which the Madrid European Council requested of the Commission. The document attempts to explain the way the Commission has considered the various applications for membership, the main issues raised by those applications and the time-table for starting negotiations. It draws the main conclusions and recommendations from the Opinions and presents the Commission's views on the issues relating to enlargement that arise for all applicant countries as well as the strengthening of the preaccession strategy.

The following extracts from COM(97) 2000, Vol. II deal with:

A. The principal questions which arise for all applicant countries on the way to enlargement

B. The strategy for enlargement, including accession negotiations and the strengthening of the preaccession strategy

C. Final recommendations.

A. PRINCIPAL QUESTIONS

Enlargement to some 25 countries and 475 million inhabitants will bring considerable political and economic advantages, and will further Union policies if certain conditions are met.

Enlargement will, however, bring greater heterogeneity to the Union and some sectoral and regional adjustment problems will result. These could limit the benefits of enlargement and make more difficult the further development of the *acquis* unless adequate preparations are made.

It is vital to use the preaccession period to the full to ensure that the applicants make adequate preparations for membership. This will require substantial investment in sectors such as the environment, transport, energy, industrial restructuring, agricultural infrastructure and rural society. The funds needed will have to come from public and private sources in the applicant countries themselves, the Union and other providers of foreign capital. Standards among the applicant countries are generally low in the social sphere, in particular in the areas of public health, unemployment and health and safety at work. Too slow an adaptation of their standards could undermine the unitary character of the *acquis* and possibly distort the operation of the single market. Supporting the process of adaptation will be necessary in the reinforced preaccession strategy.

1. *Agriculture*

In most of the candidate countries currently important price gaps (in the sense of lower prices than in the EU) exist for the main commodities. In the crop sector these vary from around 10–30 per cent for cereals, oil-seeds and protein crops to 40–50 per cent for sugar beet (although for sugar the price gap is generally somewhat smaller) and in the livestock sector from 30–40 per cent for milk and dairy products to 35–45 per cent for beef. For the cereals based meats (pigmeat and poultry) price differences are relatively small. For certain fruit and vegetables important price differences exist (e.g. up to 80 per cent for tomatoes). A further increase in producer prices in these countries can be expected from here towards the middle of the next period of financial perspectives, which will somewhat reduce, but not eliminate the price gaps.

By then, the gaps for cereals and beef may have largely disappeared if the proposed reforms are carried out. For sugar and dairy and certain fruit and vegetables price gaps in the order of 20 to 30 per cent or higher can still be expected to exist in the medium term. For the sugar and dairy-processing industries in these countries overnight price alignment (i.e. full integration into CAP from day one) would imply an important hike in their raw material price, while at the same time facing the full competitive pressure from the Single Market. Introduction of quotas would counteract the tendency to increase sugar beet and milk production under influence of the higher producer prices. Domestic demand could be expected to be negatively affected, increasing sugar and dairy surpluses in these countries. For certain fruit and vegetables, immediate integration in the CAP would provoke market imbalances.

The primary sector in candidate countries with a relatively large average size of holdings, in particular in the arable crop sector, would face relatively few problems in integrating into the CAP market and price policy. In the livestock sector such integration will take longer, in view of the capital investments, restructuring and the reorganization of management still needed. In some candidate countries agricultural structures are weaker due to the much smaller average farm size.

In the downstream sectors, including the first processing stage, large efforts in restructuring and modernization remain necessary in all countries, although those countries with relatively large foreign investment in the food processing industry would seem to be more advanced. Adjustment pressure on the CEEC food industry when entering the Single Market is expected to be large, in particular in those industries faced with increases in raw material prices and in those countries with a weak primary sector.

The weakness of their farm sector and agrifood industry and the foreseeable price differentials make it necessary to envisage for most of the applicant countries a transition period that could vary in length according to the country concerned. Such a transition period would make it possible to cushion the shock of price adjustment to the extent necessary and would avoid exposing the applicant countries' processing industry to excessive competition. In all events, there would be no need during this period to provide direct income support such as that resulting from the 1992 CAP reform. On the other hand, the applicant countries should be able to receive aid for developing their agricultural and processing structures in order to gradually prepare them for full integration into the common agricultural market.

2. *Cohesion Policy*

The continued commitment to economic and social cohesion which results from the first part of this communication implies that new Member States as of accession will progressively—and in line with their absorption capacity—benefit from the cofinancing under the Union's structural policies. Towards the end of the next period of financial perspectives (2000–2006) it would thus be possible that financial transfers from the structural policies would be comparable to those attributed to Union Member States lagging behind in their development.

It is of the utmost importance to familiarize the applicant countries with the structural policies' principles and procedures in order to prepare them before accession for the progressive introduction of Union structural policies. To this effect—in the context of the enhanced preaccession strategy—applicant countries should benefit from preaccession assistance to prepare themselves.

It should also be pointed out that the high level of cofinancing by the Cohesion Fund (85 per cent) should permit from the outset of accession and given the existence of a convergence programme, financing of important projects in such sectors as environment and trans-European networks [TENs]which are crucial to their integration into the Union.

3. *Implementing the Single Market*

A fully operating Single Market is of crucial importance to the new Member States as it offers potential for growth and jobs. Hence the importance of applying in advance of accession all the elements of the White Paper on the Single Market, through a specific procedure. Only then a full application of a Single Market without border controls is conceivable.

Possible difficulties related to trade in agricultural products or to free movement of workers and of persons in general should not prevent the full implementation by the candidate countries of the measures foreseen in the White Paper related to the abolition of border controls.

4. *Implementing Environmental Standards*

Environment is a major challenge for enlargement: while the adoption of the Union's environmental rules and standards is essential, none of the candidate countries can be expected to comply fully with the *acquis* in the near future, given their present environmental problems and the need for massive investments.

These problems are far more severe than those faced by present Member States. The persistence of a gap between levels of environmental protection in present and new members would distort the functioning of the Single Market and could lead to a protectionist reaction. This situation would affect the Union's capability to develop its environmental policy.

Nonetheless, effective compliance with Union environmental standards would necessitate, apart from important legislative and administrative efforts, massive investment in the ten applicant countries. Such levels of investment would appear unsustainable for national budgets even in the long term. The Union will not be in a position to cover the resulting financing gap by the time of enlargement. Investment for the adoption of the *acquis*, however, is one of the priorities of the reinforced preaccession strategy, and forms the basis of the reorientation of Phare.

This apparent impasse can be tackled through a two-fold approach:

- In partnership with the Union, realistic national long-term strategies for gradual effective alignment should be drawn up and start being implemented in all applicant countries before accession, in particular for tackling water and air pollution. These strategies should identify key priority areas and objectives to be fulfilled by the dates of accession as well as timetables for further full compliance; ensuing obligations should be incorporated in the accession treaties. All new investments should comply with the *acquis*.
- Important domestic and foreign financial resources, in particular from the private sector, will have to be mobilized in support of these strategies. The Union will be able to make only a partial contribution.

5. *Transport*

Very important investment in the applicants' transport infrastructure will have to be made, to avoid bottlenecks resulting from increasing flows and to allow for the full benefits of integration to be reaped. Development of transport infrastructure is also likely to be a high priority for the applicant countries themselves. Investment needs in transport infrastructure will be very high and an important part will have to be financed from sources other than national budgets. Substantial support will be needed from the Union for TEN-related corridors.

Full adaptation to Union safety and other technical norms will be necessary for a smooth enlargement. On the whole, operators should be able to bear the cost of gradual adaptation involving substantial renewal of fleets. However, specific measures might be needed, mainly in the railway sector, to encourage a favourable modal development in line with the orientations of the Common Transport Policy, and to address the consequences of restructuring.

6. *Nuclear Safety*

The nuclear industry accounts for 30 per cent of electricity-generation in the applicant countries, on average, and as much as 80 per cent in some countries. Most of the power stations were built using Soviet technology and do not meet international safety standards.

The solution is not simply to close them down, as they do not all pose the same risk and the cost of obtaining alternative energy supplies would be extremely high. Several of the applicant countries have already begun constructing new nuclear power plants, which they consider the least expensive way of meeting growth-led energy demand and of achieving independence in the energy sector.

The Union must protect the life and health of its present and future citizens. This implies that the applicants should co-operate fully in efforts to bring their levels of nuclear safety up to international standards, in accordance with the approach of the G7 since 1992. This implies that:

- Where western-designed nuclear plants are in use (Romania and Slovenia), developments should be monitored to ensure that operations comply with the appropriate safety standards. Technical assistance can be provided if necessary.
- Where the safety of Soviet-designed nuclear power stations, which are in operation or under construction, can be upgraded to meet international safety standards, modernization programmes should be fully implemented over a period of 7–10 years. (This applies to Dukovny and Temelin in the Czech Republic, Paks in Hungary, and certain units at Bohunice and Mochovce in Slovakia and at Kozloduy in Bulgaria.) The timetables agreed by the governments concerned, subject to certain conditions, for the closure of non-upgradeable units must be respected. (This applies to Bohunice in Slovakia, Ignalina in Lithuania and certain units at Kozloduy in Bulgaria.) Meanwhile, the urgent improvements called for by international experts should be carried out.

The plant closure commitments given by Bulgaria and Lithuania in return for loans granted by the EBRD/Nuclear Safety Account were subject to certain conditions. The Nuclear Safety Account Agreement entered into in 1993 by Bulgaria provided for the closure of the four units concerned at Kozloduy as soon as other duly specified energy sources became available. The necessary work was to be completed by the end of 1998; this timing having slipped, it is now thought that units 1 and 2 could be closed in 2001 and units 3 and 4 in 2001/2002. The Nuclear Safety Account Agreement concluded in 1994 with Lithuania for the closure of two units at Ignolina provided for the first to close in 1998 and the second in 2002; however, their operation could be extended until 2004 and 2008 at the latest if certain criteria were fulfilled.

Slovakia has not taken on any international commitments concerning the closure of the two reactors concerned at Bohunice, but the government adopted a resolution in 1994 whereby these reactors would be closed down by the year 2000 at the latest if the two new units under construction at Mochovce have in the meantime entered into commercial operation.

Agreement should be reached as soon as possible between the institutions providing financial support and each of the countries concerned on the earliest practical date for the closure of the nuclear power stations in question and a support programme to make their closure possible. These programmes should be prepared by the EBRD, together with Phare, Euratom and the World Bank, which should coordinate closely.

Such coordination should be extended to all assistance and modernization operations. Given the amounts in question (some 4–5 billion ecus for the main operations over ten years), the Union will be able to make only a partial contribution.

The Union should cooperate closely with the safety authorities of the countries concerned to create a climate favourable to nuclear safety, and should support their independence vis-à-vis the political authorities.

7. *Freedom, Security and Justice*

Justice and Home Affairs became part of the Union's agenda with the entry into force of the Treaty of Maastricht. The Treaty of Amsterdam transfers some of these areas into Community competence and reinforces cooperation in the residual third pillar areas. It moreover integrates the Schengen Agreements into the Treaty on the European Union. All applicant countries are to a varying degree confronted with the challenges of the fight against organized crime, terrorism, trafficking in women and drugs.

The control of external frontiers and respect for international norms in fields such as asylum, visas and immigration brings an added dimension. The geographical situation of some of the applicants exposes them to risks of importing problems from their neighbours.

The impact of these factors on the present Union is already apparent. But the enlargement of the Union provides an opportunity to address more effectively common problems in these fields which affect both the present Union and the applicants.

Some applicant countries began determined reforms in this area early on. Others have experienced delays notably due to changes in government. Overall, their achievements both in legal terms and in practical implementation varies considerably. However the lack of trained and experienced manpower is a common feature.

In these fields institution building in the preaccession period will also be of utmost importance.

8. *Border Disputes*

Enlargement should not mean importing border conflicts. The prospect of accession acts as a powerful incentive for the states concerned to settle any border disputes. The Stability Pact promoted by the Union between May 1994 and March 1995 has also been influential in this regard. Today several disputes, of low intensity, among applicants remain to be resolved.

The dispute between Hungary and Slovakia over the dam on the Danube is before the International Court of Justice, while the question of the maritime frontier between Lithuania and Latvia is in the process of being settled. Some of the applicant countries also have unresolved disputes with third countries. The Commission considers that, before accession, applicants should make every effort to resolve any outstanding border dispute among themselves or involving third countries. Failing this they should agree that the dispute be referred to the International Court of Justice.

In any event, all candidate countries should therefore, before accession negotiations are completed, commit themselves to submit unconditionally to compulsory jurisdiction, including advance ruling of the International Court of Justice in any present or future disputes of this nature, as Hungary and Slovakia have already done in the above mentioned disagreement.

9. *Applying Community Rules in Advance of Accession*

The applicant countries must abide by commitments they have made in the framework of the WTO and the OECD. But there have been a number of disputes between the Union and certain applicant countries, in cases where the latter have put international rules, such as the most favoured nation clause or certain trade arrangements, above the provisions of the Europe Agreements and their future obligations as Member States. Such an approach is contrary to the spirit of gradual adoption of the *acquis communautaire*. Stepping up the preaccession strategy should therefore include finding solutions to these problems.

The application before accession of certain Community rules on competition and state aid is also needed. This implies that the Commission should be asked to approve or, in any event, be consulted on national decisions by the authorities in the applicant countries.

B. A STRATEGY FOR ENLARGEMENT

Negotiations will define the terms and conditions on which each of the applicant countries accede to the Union. As in the past, the basis for accession will be the *acquis* of the Union as it exists at the time of enlargement. While transition periods of definite and reasonable duration may be necessary in certain justified cases, the objective of the Union should be that the new members apply the *acquis* on accession.

This will ensure a balance of rights and obligations. The new members should accept the basic obligations on accession, otherwise their right to participate fully in the decision-making process may be put in question. The Union should not envisage any kind of second-class membership or opt-outs. Good preparation for membership, on the part of all the applicant countries, is therefore of fundamental importance. The actual timetable for accession will depend primarily on the progress made by individual countries in adopting, implementing and enforcing the *acquis*. This should continue, and be accelerated, in parallel with accession negotiations.

A successful strategy for enlargement thus needs to combine:

- negotiations, based on the principle that the *acquis* will be applied on accession;
- a reinforced preaccession strategy, for all applicant countries, designed to ensure that they take on as much as possible of the *acquis* in advance of membership.

1. *Accession Negotiations*

Principles. The position to be presented by the Union to the applicant countries with which negotiations are opened should be based on the following principles:

- new members will take on the rights and obligations of membership on the basis of the *acquis* as it exists at the time of accession;
- they will be expected to apply, implement and enforce the *acquis* upon accession; in particular, the measures necessary for the extension of the Single Market should be applied immediately;
- transition measures—but not derogations—may be agreed in the course of negotiations, in duly justified cases; they should ensure the progressive integration of the new members into the Union within a limited period of time;
- during the accession negotiations, the applicants' progress in adopting the *acquis* and in other preparations for membership will be regularly reviewed on the basis of reports from the Commission.

The negotiations will begin with the screening of secondary legislation by the Commission and each of the applicant countries with which negotiations have been opened. This preliminary stage will identify the main problem areas for subsequent negotiation.

In the last accession negotiations, which took place with particularly well-prepared applicant countries, difficulties occurred in the conduct of four separate, but parallel, accession conferences of an intergovernmental nature. The Union's arrangements for the future accession negotiations will need to take full account of the complexity of the matters involved, the degree of preparation of the applicant countries, and the need for overall coherence with the reinforced preaccession strategy.

Transition Periods. In its interim report on enlargement to the Madrid European Council, the Commission indicated that the basis for accession is the *acquis* of the Union, as it exists at the time, but that transitional arrangements may be needed in some areas such as agriculture and free movement of persons. Any transition periods should, however, be limited both in scope and duration.

2. *Reinforcing the Preaccession Strategy*

At the request of the Dublin European Council, the Commission is proposing the reinforcement of the preaccession strategy for all CEEC applicant countries, whatever the stage they have reached in the transition process. This will enable assistance to be directed towards the specific needs of each applicant, with a view to the negotiations, in a coherent overall approach. In this way, the Union will be able to provide support for overcoming particular problems identified in the opinions, without the need for long transition periods which would put into question the *acquis* and the economic and social cohesion of the Union as a whole.

The reinforced preaccession strategy outlined below has two main objectives. First, to bring together the different forms of support provided by the Union within a single framework, the Accession Partnerships, and to work together with the applicants, within this framework, on the basis of a clearly defined programme to prepare for membership, involving commitments by the applicants to particular priorities and to a calendar for carrying them out; secondly, to familiarize the applicants with Union policies and procedures, through the possibility of their participation in Community programmes.

The existing preaccession strategy is founded on the Europe Agreements, the White Paper on the Single Market, the structured dialogue and Phare.

In the light of the intensity of contacts between the Union and the applicants during the coming phase of the accession process, in the framework of the negotiations, the Europe Agreements and the Accession Partnerships, the present structured dialogue no longer appears appropriate.

Most accession-related issues of principal concern to the Union and the applicants will be discussed bilaterally. In the event that accession-related issues of a horizontal nature arise which could advantageously be taken up in a multilateral framework, an ad hoc dialogue could be arranged for this purpose by the Presidency and the Commission with the ten Central and Eastern European countries. This approach should enable the dialogue to focus on such issues with a minimum of formality.

Pre-accession Aid. In addition to Phare (ecu 1.5 billion per year), the preaccession aid to be granted to the applicant CEECs from the year 2000 will consist of two elements:

- aid for agricultural development amounting to ecu 500 million a year;
- structural aid amounting to ecu 1 billion. This aid would be directed mainly towards aligning these applicant countries on Community infrastructure standards, particularly—and by analogy with the assistance currently provided under the Cohesion Fund—in the transport and environmental spheres. It would also familiarize these countries with the arrangements for implementing structural measures.

Accession Partnerships. The new instrument of the Accession Partnership will be the key feature of the reinforced strategy and will mobilize all forms of assistance to the applicant countries in central and eastern Europe within a single framework for the implementation of national programmes to prepare them for membership of the Union.

Accession Partnerships would involve:

- precise commitments on the part of the applicant country, relating in particular to democracy, macro-economic stabilization and nuclear safety, as well as a national programme for the adoption of the Community *acquis* within a precise timetable, focusing on the priority areas identified in each opinion;
- mobilization of all resources available to the Community for preparing the applicant countries for accession. This means first and foremost the Phare programme but also any new forms of assistance that the Community could provide in the context of future financial perspectives. Other resources could be mobilized from international financial institutions for work on standards and the development of SMEs [Small and Medium-sized Enterprises]. Phare could be used as a catalyst for cofinancing operations with the EIB [European Investment Bank], the EBRD [European Bank for Reconstruction and Development] and the World Bank with whom the Commission will conclude framework agreements. Given the enormous requirements, in particular in the field of environment and transport, the Commission suggests that around 70 per cent of the Phare funds be used for investment.

The programme for adopting the *acquis* would be drawn up with the Commission in partnership with each of the applicant countries. The priorities set should initially correspond to the sectors identified as deficient in the opinions. Work towards the objectives would be covered by an indicative timetable. The granting of assistance—on the basis of annual financing agreements—will be conditional on achieving these objectives and on progress made. Implementation of the programme would thus depend on strict 'accession conditionality' based on suitable evaluation mechanisms and a continuous dialogue with the Commission.

The Commission would regularly report on progress to the European Council. The first report will be submitted at the end of 1998 and then on an annual basis thereafter. The progress of the applicant countries in fulfilling the targets set out in each individual Accession Partnership will serve as the basis of the reports. When an applicant country is judged to have fulfilled the necessary conditions to enter into accession negotiations and has not already done so, the Commission will forward a recommendation to the Council that accession negotiations should be launched.

Each Accession Partnership will take the form of a Commission decision to be taken after consulting the applicant country concerned and with due regard to the opinions of the management committees involved in administering assistance which has hitherto been granted from a range of different sources.

Preparation of the Accession Partnerships will begin in the second half of 1997.

Participation in Community Programmes and Mechanisms to Apply the acquis. As the applicant countries progressively adopt the *acquis* in preparation for membership, they should be given an opportunity to participate in Community programmes.

This is provided for in the Europe Agreements and does not raise problems of principle. As these programmes encompass most Community policies, covering education, training, research, culture, environment, SMEs and the Single Market, they will provide a useful preparation for accession in familiarizing the applicant countries and their citizens with the Union's policies and working methods.

The problem is to make this participation effective for all programmes. It will be necessary, depending on the budgetary resources of each country, to permit the Phare programme to cofinance the applicant countries' participation in the programmes beyond the 10 per cent assistance limit laid down by the European Council in Essen.

The gradual integration of the Central and Eastern European countries into the different programmes will enable their representatives to become more familiar with Community legislation and proceedings and to take advantage of Member States' experience in areas such as public procurement, the right of residence and VAT [value-added tax]. Nevertheless, this does not imply giving decision-making power to countries which are not yet members of the Union.

The involvement of certain Community agencies or bodies will also help better prepare the adoption of the *acquis*. More frequent contacts within these bodies will enable certain problems to be resolved at a technical level. A special effort will be made to familiarize the applicants with Community agencies, such as the Medicines Evaluation and the Environment Agency, the European Statistical Office (Eurostat), and the Veterinary and Phytosanitary Office, and with certification and standardization bodies.

The European Conference. Enlargement is a long-term process affecting the whole of Europe. The Member States of the Union and all those European countries aspiring to membership and linked to it through an association agreement should be brought together in a single forum.

The European Conference would provide an opportunity for consultations on a broad range of issues arising in the areas of the Common Foreign and Security Policy [CFSP] and Justice and Home Affairs.

With regard to the CFSP, the conference would provide a framework for dialogue on international problems of common concern, such as relations with Russia, Ukraine and other CIS countries and European security. The conference would enable participating countries to be involved more closely in the preparation and implementation of joint actions, declarations and demarches. This would contribute to the overall weight and coherence of decisions and actions taken under the CFSP.

In the field of Justice and Home Affairs, the Union and the other participants in the conference share many concerns in areas including the fight against organized crime, terrorism, corruption, drug trafficking, illegal arms sales, money laundering and illegal immigration. The European Conference would facilitate cooperation between national authorities, including police and judicial officials, and cooperation with Europol.

The Conference would meet each year at the level of Heads of State or Government and the President of the Commission and, where necessary, ministerial level.

C. FINAL RECOMMENDATIONS

1. The Commission invites the Council to endorse the approach to the challenge of enlargement set out in this communication.

    Enlargement, as the Amsterdam European Council indicated, is an inclusive process embracing all of the applicant countries. The overall process includes the opening of accession negotiations with individual countries, according to the stage which each has reached in satisfying the basic conditions of membership and in preparing for accession; and an accompanying framework which consists of the reinforcement of the preaccession strategy for countries of Central and Eastern Europe, as well as the creation of a multilateral forum of cooperation in the form of a European Conference.

2. As regards the opening of accession negotiations, the European Council has already concluded that they should commence with Cyprus six months after the end of the Intergovernmental Conference.

3. Concerning the countries of Central and Eastern Europe, the Commission has now presented in its Opinions an objective analysis, in the light of the criteria laid down by the Copenhagen European Council. The Commission considers that none of them fully satisfy all the criteria at the present time. However, nine countries satisfy the political conditions, while certain countries have made sufficient progress towards satisfying the economic conditions and those related to the other obligations of membership.

In the light of its analysis, and in accordance with their respective merits, the Commission considers that Hungary, Poland, Estonia, the Czech Republic and Slovenia could be in a position to satisfy all the conditions of membership in the medium term if they maintain and strongly sustain their efforts of preparation.

The Commission underlines that a decision to open accession negotiations simultaneously with the countries mentioned does not imply that negotiations will be concluded simultaneously. The timing of the conclusions of accession negotiations will depend in large part on the accomplishment of the further efforts required from each applicant country in the respective Opinions.

4. On this basis, the Commission recommends the Council to open negotiations with the following countries (listed in chronological order of their accession requests): Hungary, Poland, Estonia, the Czech Republic and Slovenia.

5. As regards the reinforcement of the preaccession strategy, the Union is firmly committed to working with each of the CEEC applicant countries, notably through the Accession Partnerships, to overcome the difficulties which they face in preparation for membership, and which are identified in the Opinions. The Commission will report regularly to the European Council on the progress made. The first report will be submitted at the end of 1998 and then on an annual basis thereafter. The progress of the applicant countries in fulfilling the targets set out in each individual Accession Partnership will serve as the basis of the reports. When an applicant country is judged to have fulfilled the necessary conditions to enter into accession negotiations and has not already done so, the Commission will forward a recommendation to the Council that accession negotiations should be launched.

6. In place of the existing structured dialogue, multilateral meetings with the applicant countries of Central and Eastern Europe could be

arranged by the Presidency and the Commission to discuss accession-related issues other than those arising in the individual accession negotiations.

7. The overall framework should be completed by the creation of a European Conference, to address issues related to cooperation in the fields of Common Foreign and Security Policy, and Justice and Home Affairs; the Conference would comprise the Member States of the Union and all those European countries aspiring to membership and linked to it through an association agreement (COM (97) 2000 Vol. II, pp. 47-57).

7 |

Reactions to Agenda 2000

This chapter describes the reactions to Agenda 2000, and more particularly its recommendations on enlargement, from the applicant countries, and on the Union's side among the Member States and in the Council, the Parliament and the other institutions.

The general reaction in the Union was favourable. The Commission had seized the initiative at a good moment, just after the relative disappointment of the Intergovernmental Conference, with a long-term plan that set the agenda for decisions over a number of years. Since the immediate decisions, to be taken by the end of 1997, concerned enlargement, the focus of discussion was on that, rather than on agriculture, the financial framework or the structural framework, on which decisions would not be taken until formal proposals were tabled in 1998. But the overall articulation of the package, and its realism in budgetary terms, were well received: with the emphasis at national levels on limiting public deficits, in line with the convergence criteria for Economic and Monetary Union, a more ambitious financial proposal for an increase in the budgetary ceiling at the European level would not have been viable. There were, however, already warnings of the difficulties in store for the substantial discussions on agriculture and the structural funds, once the formal proposals in these fields were on the table.

Even for enlargement, the decisions to be taken immediately were of a procedural nature (opening of negotiations), or for the strengthening of the preaccession strategy: difficult decisions relating to the substance of the accession negotiations and the timing of enlargement were left until later.

On all sides, both in the Union and among the candidates, there was a positive reaction to the quality of the analysis in the Opinions; their comprehensive nature, and their degree of detail, were perhaps a surprise to those who had studied previous Opinions, which had dealt with a range of topics more limited than the Copenhagen criteria. But, not surprisingly, the differentiation proposed by the Commission—the recommendation to open negotiations immediately with five countries of Central and Eastern Europe, together with Cyprus (the '5 plus 1' formula)—caused disappointment on the part of the other five applicant countries, and discussion within the Union. Consequently, it was on the question of differentiation that the political debate largely focused in the autumn of 1997.

The Applicant Countries

In their immediate reactions to the Opinions, in the days which followed publication, the five applicant countries for which the Commission recommended opening accession negotiations were, naturally, positive. The five other candidates, particularly the two Baltic states, Latvia and Lithuania, expressed their disappointment.

The full texts of each of their Opinions, and of Agenda 2000, were given to the Ambassadors of the ten countries by the Commissioner responsible, Hans van den Broek, at a brief meeting at Strasbourg in the morning of 16 July, before they were presented to the Parliament and press. They were made available both in paper form and on diskette, for rapid electronic transmission to capitals. Since they had been sent electronically on the previous day to the Commission's delegations in the countries concerned, they were available at press conferences held in most of the ten capitals on 16 July. It was difficult for the governments of the applicant countries to give a considered reaction to a document of more than a hundred pages, available only in a foreign language. It was not until some weeks later that the Opinions were translated into their languages. Consequently, their first reactions were based on a very rapid reading, probably only of the summary and conclusion of their Opinion, which led to misunderstandings. In the case of Latvia, the economic indicators quoted in the summary of the Opinion are limited to 1996, without mention of more favourable recent developments (for example, the decline in inflation in the early months of 1997) which figure elsewhere in the text; so one of Latvia's first public reactions was to criticize the Commission for using outdated statistical data, and for neglecting other important elements, which put in question the objectiveness of its conclusions.

In both Latvia and Lithuania, there was surprise that Estonia had received a more favourable Opinion, and a suspicion that the recommendations had been influenced by political considerations. It was feared that the different treatment of Estonia would affect Baltic relations, and make it more difficult to maintain domestic motivation for the reform process. These negative reactions were amplified in the following weeks. Latvia's Prime Minister Krasts, speaking to a Committee of the European Parliament in Brussels in September, argued that the Opinions showed that the differences between the candidates were not so substantial as to determine with exactitude their compliance with the Copenhagen criteria, and warned about the consequences of public frustration in the countries left out of negotiations; because the political aspects of accession were of the utmost importance, the only appropriate solution was a simultaneous start to negotiations. Lithuania's Prime Minister Vagnorius warned a meeting of the European Parliament's Christian Democrats in Stockholm in September that barring his country and Latvia from the first wave of enlargement could stoke security tensions in the Baltic region and create 'new dividing lines in Europe'; he argued that Lithuania's exclusion from the chosen five was based on political considerations and lacked objectivity, and the Commission had used outdated economic statistics when making its assessment. A Latvian diplomat was quoted as saying: 'What we want is to be on the train from the beginning; if we are not, it would give an indication that the EU still regards us as within the Russian sphere of influence.'

In Romania, the official reaction to the Opinion was to contest its conclusions. Prime Minister Ciorbea said at a news conference on 16 July that 'expansion by waves is justified in the case of NATO, but is not justified for EU enlargement, which is a process of continuous integration; we will continue our political and diplomatic fight right through until December for the adoption of a political decision on EU expansion!' In a more measured reaction a few days later, the Foreign Ministry accepted that 'in its broad lines, the Commission's Opinion corresponds to the reality of today's Romania' but argued that 'to separate the applicant countries into two groups for the opening of negotiations is counterproductive, creating artificial and discriminatory frontiers, contrary to the principle of continuity of the process of enlargement of the EU; this method would penalize Romania, and could influence public opinion negatively and slow down the rate of economic reform'. Romania's campaign of persuasion continued in the following months. In a paper distributed in November 1997, it added further arguments against differentiation: it would distort trade, lead to discrimination between applicant countries in terms of financial transfers (the six countries of the 'first group' would obtain much more from the European budget in the period 2000–2006 than the other five), and cause a 'massive migration of foreign direct investment' to countries of the first group. But, by this time, Romania realized that the Commission's basic recommendations were likely to be accepted, and argued for enlargement to be made more inclusive by underlining the importance of the European Conference, the Accession Partnerships, and the annual review of progress for each candidate, alongside negotiations with candidates who have made significant progress. Romania even conceded that 'the first candidates to enter this stage may be those recommended by the Commission'.

Bulgaria's initial reactions were more muted. The Foreign Minister commented to the press on 16 July that the Opinion did not contain negative components, but was an expression of the EU's willingness to help countries seeking membership; the media expressed disappointment, but accepted that much time had been wasted in previous years due to lack of reforms. Officially, the Bulgarian government stated a few days later that 'the Opinion provides an important reference for the lagging behind of Bulgaria in terms of commitment to market-oriented economic policy, land reform, privatization and the development of a dynamic private sector. This limited progress is the result of lack of action and wrong policy decisions in the recent years.' It went on to argue that 'a decision by the European Council to launch simultaneous negotiations would be a recognition of the principle of equal starting opportunities for all applicant countries to be part of the united Europe'.

Slovakia's official reaction to the Opinion was restrained. It can hardly have been a surprise that the Commission's evaluation on the political criteria was negative, in view of the demarches already made to Slovakia by the Union, and the warnings given by many European politicians. Prime Minister Meciar downplayed the importance of the Opinion, indicating that the final decision would be taken by the European Council, and that the Slovak opposition and press had to share the blame for the exclusion of Slovakia from the group of candidates for membership negotiations. In subsequent contacts with the Commission, the Slovak government argued that the Opinion contained inaccuracies, was not objective and that the Commission had applied double standards: on the political criteria, Slovakia was not significantly different from other 'transitional' countries. In Slovakia it became clear that in advance of the 1998 elections (presidential and parliamentary) the opposition parties were not willing to cooperate with the government to carry through political reforms. Despite some positive signs, such as a joint declaration on European questions in October by President and Prime Minister, none of the deficiencies mentioned in the political chapter of the Opinion were addressed: the language law for the Hungarian minority did not materialize, with the Slovak government arguing that it was not necessary; and tension with Hungary rose as a result of the alleged proposal by Prime Minister Meciar for a population exchange between Hungarians in Slovakia and Slovakians in Hungary.

The other five candidates were, naturally, positive in their immediate reactions to the Commission's recommendations. Poland and Hungary welcomed the judgment. Estonia expressed 'gratitude' to the Commission for its thorough and objective work. Slovenia said that the recommendation to include it in negotiations would encourage it to accelerate its preparation for them. Hungary's Foreign Minister was happy about the positive evaluation in the Opinion, but emphasized the need to catch up with the arrears mentioned in its critical observations.

All the applicant countries, with the exception of Hungary, sent to the Commission in due course a written commentary on the Opinions, those of Latvia and Lithuanian being particularly rapid and detailed, and most of these commentaries were also sent to the authorities of the Member States. Although a number of errors of detail were noted, and the commentaries listed new legislative or economic developments subsequent to the finalization of the Opinions, the Commission came to the conclusion that there was no reason to issue a modification or correction of any part of the Opinions.

As the debate on the Opinions proceeded, and the arguments in favour of a common start were voiced by the disappointed candidates and in influential circles on the Union side, the other candidates began to speak up in favour of the differentiation proposed by the Commission. Hungary's Prime Minister Horn said in September that to open negotiations with all the candidates would 'demoralize the states that were prepared and were showing results'. In November, Hungary's ambassador to the EU asked 'what then would all the work done, and all the sacrifices asked of the population during the past eight or nine years, amount to?' and 'which of the two solutions would be politically trickier: not inviting some countries to negotiations from the start, or telling them at some point that things cannot continue and they must stop negotiations?'

The Commission responded to the arguments for a common start by restating and explaining the strategy of Agenda 2000. In an article in September in the press (*Financial Times*, 22 September 1997), the commissioner responsible, Hans Van den Broek, said:

> The idea that the EU is drawing new dividing lines across Europe is a red herring. There are no 'ins and outs', but rather 'ins and pre-ins'. As with economic and monetary union, proper preparation is crucial. Agenda 2000 confirms that we will work with each country to help it prepare for membership. An extra effort will be made through targeted support to help the 'pre-ins' overcome remaining problems.
>
> Some advocate a common start to the negotiations with all applicants, whatever their preparedness for membership. But little, beyond momentary political satisfaction, would be gained by opening negotiations with countries that are insufficiently prepared. Negotiations would soon become bogged down, leading to disenchantment. The superficial appeal of a common starting line would quickly fade if the whole enlargement process and the progress of the more advanced applicants were held back. The Commission carefully considered these questions as well as the interests of our own citizens in a properly planned enlargement before unanimously recommending that negotiations begin next year with the five most advanced countries in the region, plus Cyprus.
>
> At the same time we propose to double 'preaccession' assistance for all the applicants in central and eastern Europe. Countries not yet ready to start negotiations will benefit without discrimination from this support. Indeed, they will receive increasing amounts of assistance as other candidates become members and the total amount available for preaccession is shared out among fewer beneficiaries.
>
> The EU will monitor progress in overcoming the problems. As soon as a candidate has fulfilled conditions set out by our heads of government, the Commission will recommend that enlargement negotiations start. This is not merely 'leaving the door open' but a firm commitment.
>
> I fully understand the disappointment in countries that have recently committed themselves to long overdue political and economic reforms and are now making strides in the right direction. Some 'pre-ins' contend that investment in their country will suffer if they are not included in a first wave of negotiations. But investors base their decisions on hard-headed estimates of potential returns and not on the date when a complex political negotiation begins.

The Agenda 2000 recommendations provide every opportunity for catching up and do not prejudge the date when any candidate will join. This will largely depend on the efforts each country is willing and able to make.

The Member States

The Member States of the Union, in their initial reactions in the Council of Ministers, welcomed the Commission's recommendations on enlargement in Agenda 2000. Unlike the applicant countries, they did not need to take public positions immediately, and were able to digest the voluminous documentation at technical level in capitals before embarking on discussions in the autumn. The decisions to be taken on enlargement formed part of a wider package including financial questions, agriculture and structural funds, which would remain linked to enlargement for some time to come, and this global approach was confirmed by the insistence of the Luxembourg presidency that the dossier be coordinated by one Council—the General Affairs Council, in which Member States are represented by foreign ministers, and whose deliberations are prepared by the Committee of Permanent Representations (COREPER)—at a series of meetings at which Agenda 2000 figured as a constant item on the agenda. Although the views of other specialist Councils—the agriculture ministers and the economic and finance ministers (ECOFIN)—were also sought, the decisions to be taken at the top level at the European Council in Luxembourg on 12–13 December 1997 were prepared by the General Affairs Council.

The discussion of enlargement among Member States reflected the network of special relations which had grown up between the existing members and the future members—in some cases, almost a 'patron–client' relationship. This phenomenon is not new in the context of enlargement: in most previous enlargements, there have been existing members more favourably disposed to particular candidates, for broad political reasons or for specific reasons of economic interest, and to whom the candidates have looked for advice and support. But the larger number of countries under consideration on this occasion—ten countries of Central and Eastern Europe, plus Cyprus—has made for an even more complicated series of relationships.

The interest of Member States in applicant countries is generally determined by geographical proximity, coupled with the historical links to which geography has given rise. For example, Austria tends to be interested particularly in the accession of its immediate neighbours, Slovenia, Hungary, Slovakia and the Czech Republic, all of which were involved in Austria's history. Germany tends to be interested in the accession of Poland, the Czech Republic, Slovakia and Hungary, which lie on its eastern frontiers, forming the zone between it and the former Soviet Union. Italy has close links with its neighbour Slovenia. Greece is interested not only in the accession of Cyprus, but also of Bulgaria and Romania because of their role in the Balkan region. The three Nordic Member States (Denmark, Sweden, Finland) are interested in the accession of their Baltic neighbours (Lithuania, Latvia, Estonia) and a north–south correlation can even be discerned between these two groups, with close economic links between Finland and its neighbour Estonia, Swedish interest in Latvia, and Danish interest in Lithuania. Other Member States, being at a greater distance, tend to have less pronounced links, but there is also a particular cultural and political relationship between France and Romania.

The role of 'patron' is not limited to the existing Member States, but can be detected on the part of some of the applicant countries; Poland, being the biggest applicant country in Central and Eastern Europe, tends to see itself as playing a leading role in the region, with a particular geographical and historical interest in the accession of its neighbour Lithuania, while the Czech Republic is naturally interested to assure the accession of Slovakia, with which it formed for so long a single state, and with which it has close economic links.

It has been observed, with a certain degree of truth, that one can predict which candidates for EU membership (and NATO membership) will be the object of interest for a given country by taking a look at the map of Europe and seeing which candidates lie on a direct line between it and Moscow.

In the period before the Opinions, governments of Member States had been able to say, in their bilateral dialogue with the various applicant countries, that the decision on the next stage of the enlargement process—the opening of accession negotiations—would be taken only after the IGC and in the light of the Commission's analyses; during this period of 'waiting for the Opinions', Member States did not need to make firm choices between countries. The UK, for example, had been able to make strong public statements in favour of differentiation, without having to define which countries it had in mind. Now that the Opinions were on the table, Member States were obliged to show their colours and this, in diplomatic terms, promised to be a delicate exercise. Those applicant countries who were disappointed by their Opinion immediately lobbied the Member States, and looked in particular to their friends for support. This was part of the background to the discussions of EU foreign ministers during the autumn of 1997.

The Opinions themselves were subjected to detailed examination in the Council's Enlargement Group in September, with representatives of the governments of each of the 15 Member States and of the Commission, which explained each of the Opinions, and replied to questions and comments. There was no real dissent among the experts over the analyses in the Opinions, although Denmark and Sweden questioned whether they provided an adequate basis for differentiating between Estonia and the other two Baltic states. At this stage, however, most Member States were not ready to take an official position on the Commission's recommendations. During the discussions by foreign ministers which ensued, positions began to emerge. While Germany and the UK tended to agree with the Commission's recommendations, Spain, Portugal, Greece and to some extent Italy remained unconvinced, arguing in favour of a common start to negotiations for all candidates; Denmark and Sweden, disputing the differentiation between the Baltic states, also favoured a common start. In this constellation of positions, Finland's decision at an early stage to accept the Commission's recommendations, and not to join Sweden and Denmark in 'Nordic solidarity', was significant; meanwhile it was not clear to what extent the positions of Spain, Portugal and Greece, important beneficiaries of the cohesion and structural funds, were based on tactical considerations in relation to the financial part of Agenda 2000.

Although the question of differentiation continued to be an important element in the Council's discussions, it became clear that a majority was forming in favour of the Commission's recommendations, and that a solution could be found by emphasizing and reinforcing the 'inclusive' elements in the overall proposals on enlargement, with reassurances for the candidates not in the first round of negotiations.

Meanwhile other elements of Agenda 2000 were also discussed by the Council. The idea of the new Accession Partnerships with all the applicant countries was well received by Member States, in fact so well received that they insisted on a procedure whereby the principle of the Partnerships and their main lines would be approved by the Council itself, rather than by the Commission on its own.

The arrangements for the proposed European Conference were also discussed at length by the Council, including the participation of Turkey about which Greece, Germany and other Member States had reservations. Plainly, the Conference could have an important role in demonstrating the inclusiveness of the Union's approach to the applicant countries, and involving them in discussions on matters of general interest; on the other hand, the agenda for the Conference had to be limited in such a way as not to overlap with the accession negotiations, and those Member States who had reservations about Turkey wanted to limit its scope even more.

These questions were discussed at length in the General Affairs Council, at an informal meeting of foreign ministers at Mondorf-les-Bains in October, even briefly at an extraordinary meeting of heads of government (on the subject of employment) in Luxembourg in November. Decisions were not then taken, but the general lines of a solution were emerging. Commissioner Hans van den Broek reported to the European Parliament on 26 October 1997 that:

> Member States when discussing enlargement stress that it is a process from which none of the candidate countries is excluded. That means, as soon as the political and economic conditions for membership are fulfilled, membership will materialize. That is also to say—and I am echoing what all Member States agree—that enlargement includes various elements of negotiation and preparation: emphasis must lie much more clearly on the all-inclusiveness of the process and not on the fact that some would start negotiations and others would continue preparations. In that sense, one firm conclusion has been reached, namely that where differentiation is applied, it should never mean discrimination (*Agence Europe*, 27 October 1997).

There was much reflection on new 'models' for the process of enlargement. The expression 'regatta model' had been in circulation for some time, denoting the idea of a common start for all applicants (as in a yachting race) but with varying speeds and different times of finishing. Foreign Minister Kinkel, who had favoured such an approach, now replaced it by the 'stadium model', implying a limited start with the well-prepared candidates, but the possibility for other candidates to join the race at a later stage, and even catch up with the others. The Luxembourg presidency developed a 'process model' on which agreement was finally reached. This formula sought to define different layers of the 'overall enlargement process': a 'multilateral framework' bringing together Member States and all the countries aspiring to membership, including Turkey (10 plus 1 plus 1), in the European Conference; a 'single accession process' with all the applicant countries of Central and Eastern Europe and Cyprus (10 plus 1) who would benefit from the reinforced preaccession strategy; and a phase of accession negotiations, which certain candidates would enter in 1998 (5 plus 1) and others at a later stage.

European Parliament

It was to the European Parliament on 16 July that the Commission presented Agenda 2000 and the Opinions, and a lively debate ensued in the following months in the different committees of the Parliament, culminating in a resolution adopted at its session on 4 December. The Parliament's position on enlargement in this period before the opening of negotiations was important, but not decisive; it would not be until after the conclusion of negotiations that a formal consultation would take place, requiring the assent of Parliament by a two-thirds majority to the terms for enlargement. With this rendezvous in mind, Parliament will follow the process of enlargement closely, although it is not directly involved in the accession negotiations, which are intergovernmental in character. Moreover, enlargement forms part of a global package in which Parliament has a strong interest, including the development of the Union's policies and the budgetary arrangements, which touch directly on the Parliament's own powers.

Already before the presentation of Agenda 2000, the Parliament had expressed itself positively on the political aspects of enlargement, and in July 1996 there was an important meeting between the President and the presidents of the parliaments of the ten associated states of Central and Eastern Europe. In addition to these periodic collective meetings at the top level, Parliament has a continuing dialogue with all the countries concerned by means of its Joint Parliamentary Committees.

The two main strands of concern running through debates in the European Parliament on the subject of enlargement have been the need for it to be accompanied by thorough institutional reform of the Union, and concern about the budgetary implications, the majority opinion being that enlargement will, and should, result in an increase in EC expenditure. On the question of differentiation between the applicant countries, Parliament was divided. In 1996 its President, Klaus Hänsch, said that negotiations must begin simultaneously with all applicant countries 'as I cannot imagine, for political reasons, that one would choose at the beginning of 1998 the countries with which one wants to begin talks, and those that should wait still longer.'

When Agenda 2000 was presented in July 1997, there were criticisms in Parliament of the Commission's recommendations, and its choice of candidates was described by one speaker as 'arbitrary and dangerous'. In the Parliament's Foreign Affairs Committee, there was a majority in favour of a 'common start' of negotiations for all candidates, with the exception of Slovakia, for almost all parliamentarians, including the Committee's rapporteur for Slovakia, agreed with the Commission's assessment that the political conditions had not yet been satisfied for this country. The rapporteurs for the other 'disappointed' candidates (Latvia, Lithuania, Bulgaria, Romania) were in favour of the opening of negotiations with these countries. Nevertheless, the Commission's position on differentiation, explained to the Committee by the commissioner responsible, Hans van den Broek, began to be better understood, and at the same time many parliamentarians, in their dialogue with national colleagues, began to realize that a majority of Member States supported the Commission's approach.

The result was a classic parliamentary compromise. By October 1997, the Foreign Affairs Committee had examined the options and a majority in the Committee felt that it was vital to recognize the right of accession laid down in the treaties 'without creating either false hopes or frustration'. Negotiations should not be commenced with Slovakia but bilateral negotiations should open simultaneously with the other nine applicants from Central and Eastern Europe, as well as with Cyprus. Each of the negotiations would be conducted and concluded at its own pace, but negotiations with the better-prepared candidates could proceed more intensively.

> While we respect the logic of the choices which the Commission has made, we are sensitive to charges of discrimination against those countries who received a negative avis. It has been widely said that discrimination comes in two forms: it is discrimination to treat similar situations differently, but it is equally discrimination to treat different situations in the same way. The way forward is a common start followed by negotiations at different levels of intensity.

The resolution adopted by Parliament in December 1997, shortly before the European Council, followed these lines. In its resolution, Parliament

> asks the European Council to set in motion the enlargement process by a common act with all applicant countries; believes that all the applicant

countries which do at present meet the criterion of a stable democratic order, respect for human rights and the protection of minorities laid down at Copenhagen, have the right to open the reinforced accession and negotiating process at the same time, and that this process should begin for all these countries early in 1998; therefore believes that intensive negotiations on an individual basis should begin with the countries which have made the most progress and—while noting some factual inaccuracies—supports the Commission's evaluations of which these countries presently are (C4-0371/97, cited in *Agence Europe*, 5 December 1997).

It goes on to approve in general terms the other elements of the enlargement package, including the preaccession strategy, the Accession Partnerships, and the European Conference, adding that Slovakia should not be excluded from the preaccession strategy and that the Accession Partnership for Slovakia should include measures in the field of democracy.

On institutional reform, Parliament in the resolution also:

- believes that the institutional framework which has emerged from the Amsterdam Treaty does not meet the necessary conditions for achieving enlargement without endangering the operation of the Union and the effectiveness of its actions; confirms its views regarding the institutional reforms which must be achieved before any further enlargement and, in particular, repeats its calls for:
  - adjustments to be made to the weighting of votes in the Council and to the number of Commission members, with the Member States retaining equal status with each other,
  - qualified majority voting to become the general rule in the Council,
  - the requirement of unanimity to be restricted to decisions of a constitutional nature, amendments to the Treaties, accessions, decisions on own resources, electoral procedure, application of Article 308 (former 235),
  - all other reforms required for enlargement to be adopted;
- opposes the suggestion implicit in the idea that institutional reform could be postponed until the number of Member States exceeds twenty, because this idea reinforces the fear that there will be one privileged group of candidates and one with an uncertain future as to the membership.

Parliament was thus already preparing the ground for its further struggle with Council on the institutional preconditions for enlargement.

On the proposed financial framework, Parliament expressed doubts that the maintenance of the own-resources ceiling at 1.27 per cent of the Union's GDP would be possible, in view of the needs of enlargement, the difficulty of reforming the agricultural and structural funds, and the uncertainty of the hypothesis for future economic growth used by the Commission in its calculations. However, it did not suggest an alternative framework.

Other Institutions

The Economic and Social Committee, and the Committee of the Regions, also discussed the Commission's recommendations on enlargement in Agenda 2000. Although the proceedings of these other institutions are less widely reported than those of Council and Parliament, they are often well informed and percipient, and near to the concerns of the public. In the Opinion which it gave in October 1997, the Economic and Social Committee endorsed enlargement of the EU as one of the great challenges of the turn of the century, along with reform of the Treaty and Monetary Union. While welcoming the broad thrust of the Copenhagen criteria, it referred to the need to include 'conformity to the European socio-economic model' as a criterion in the assessment of the applicant countries, describing this model as 'seeking not merely to achieve formal democracy and economic efficiency, but also to bring a high degree of social acceptance, an ongoing social dialogue between the social partners and the government, and social solidarity and protection for the most vulnerable' (EcoSoc, 1997).

The Committee underlined that enlargement would bring some risks for EU Member States, such as a lower level of wages and social conditions, more employment flexibility, and difficulty in carrying forward Community policies concerning equality, labour law, and coordination of social security systems. Although it did not dissent from the Commission's assessments of the applicant countries, the Committee expressed sympathy with the 'approach advocating that negotiations should start at the same time for all applicant countries, in order to avoid a feeling of exclusion and hesitation developing among the general public in the countries concerned' (EcoSoc, 1997).

The Committee of the Regions gave its Opinion in November 1997, declaring itself resolutely in favour of enlargement provided that it did not call into question the degree of European integration already achieved. It insisted that enlargement should not be to the detriment of the less-developed regions of existing Member States, drawing attention to the fact that the regions of the Union adjacent to the applicant countries are exposed to market pressures for labour and services. The Committee underlined the risk of a large number of workers from the Central and Eastern European countries moving into Member States, and of a delocalization of industrial employment from Member States to regions of the applicant countries, where wage levels and environmental standards are lower (CdR, 1997).

The European Council, Luxembourg, 12–13 December 1997

The decisions of the European Council meeting at Luxembourg were awaited with intense interest by the candidate countries. There had been considerable lobbying by the 'pre-ins', strongly supported by Denmark and Sweden, to secure approval for the 'regatta start'. In the event, whilst underlying the inclusive nature of the enlargement process, the European Council basically followed the recommendations of the Commission in Agenda 2000. The conclusions of Luxembourg skilfully articulated this enlargement process in terms of a multilateral framework (the European Conference), a single accession process involving 11 countries, and the opening of concession negotiations in the first place with six states.

The Council decided to launch an accession process forming part of Article O of the Treaty on European Union and comprising the ten CEEC applicants and Cyprus; it confirmed that all these states are destined to join the EU on the basis of the same criteria, and participate in the accession process on the same footing. The process will be launched on 30 March 1998 at a meeting of the foreign ministers with the 11 countries concerned, within a single framework.

The European Council declared that 'enlargement is a comprehensive, inclusive and ongoing process, which will take place in stages; each of the applicant States will proceed at its own rate, depending on its degree of preparedness'. With regard to the opening of accession negotiations, bilateral intergovernmental conferences would subsequently be convened in the Spring of 1998

> to begin negotiations with Cyprus, Hungary, Poland, Estonia the Czech Republic and Slovenia on the conditions for their entry into the Union and the ensuing Treaty adjustments... At the same time, the preparation

of negotiations with Romania, Slovakia, Latvia, Lithuania and Bulgaria will be speeded up in particular through an analytical examination of the Union *acquis*.

From the end of 1998, the Commission will make regular reports to the Council, together with any necessary recommendations for opening bilateral intergovernmental conferences, reviewing the progress of each Central and East European applicant State towards accession in the light of the Copenhagen criteria, in particular the rate at which it is adopting the Union *acquis*. Prior to those reports, implementation of the accession partnerships and progress in adopting the *acquis* will be examined with each applicant State in the Europe Agreement bodies. The Commission's reports will serve as a basis for taking, in the Council context, the necessary decisions on the conduct of the accession negotiations or their extension to other applicants. In that context, the Commission will continue to follow the method adopted by Agenda 2000 in evaluating applicant States' ability to meet the economic criteria and fulfil the obligations deriving from accession (*Agence Europe*, 14 December 1997).

The European Council decided that the European Conference

will bring together the Member States of the European Union and the European States aspiring to accede to it and sharing its values and internal and external objectives. The members of the Conference must share a common commitment to peace, security and good neighbourliness, respect for other countries' sovereignty, the principles upon which the European Union is founded, the integrity and inviolability of external borders and the principles of international law and a commitment to the settlement of territorial disputes by peaceful means, in particular through the jurisdiction of the International Court of Justice in the Hague. Countries which endorse these principles and respect the right of any European country fulfilling the required criteria to accede to the European Union and sharing the Union's commitment to building a Europe free of the divisions and difficulties of the past will be invited to take part in the Conference.

Initially, the EU offer will be addressed to Cyprus, the applicant states of Central and Eastern Europe and Turkey.

The European Conference will be a multilateral forum for political consultation, intended to address questions of general concern to the participants and to broaden and deepen their cooperation on foreign and security policy, justice and home affairs, and other areas of common concern, particularly economic matters and regional cooperation. The Conference will be chaired by the State holding the Presidency of the Council of the European Union. At the Presidency's invitation, Heads of

State and Government and the President of the Commission will meet at
the Conference once a year, as will the Minister for Foreign Affairs.

The European Council also agreed on an enhanced preaccession
strategy

> to enable all the applicant States of the Central and Eastern Europe even-
> tually to become members of the European Union and, to that end, to
> align themselves as far as possible on the Union *acquis* prior to acces-
> sion. With the Europe Agreements, which remain the basis of the
> Union's relations with these States, the strategy centres on accession
> partnerships and increased preaccession aid. It will be accompanied by
> an analytical study of the Union *acquis* for each applicant State taken
> individually (*Agence Europe*, 14 December 1997).

Preaccession aid will be increased substantially; alongside the Phare
programme, which will already have been refocused on accession priorities, it will, as from the year 2000, comprise aid for agriculture and a
structural instrument which will give priority to measures similar to
those of the cohesion fund. Financial support to the countries involved
in the enlargement process will be based on the principle of equal
treatment, independently of time of accession, with particular attention
being paid to countries with the greatest need. Without prejudice to
decisions on the financial perspectives for 2000–2006, the Phare programme will focus on accession by setting two priority aims: the reinforcement of administrative and judicial capacity (about 30 per cent of
the overall amount) and investments related to the adoption and application of the *acquis* (about 70 per cent).

Some Community programmes (e.g. education, training and
research) will be open to applicant states and this will enable them to
familiarize themselves with the Union's policies and working methods.
Such participation will have to be determined case by case, with each
applicant state making a steadily increasing financial contribution of its
own. Phare will, if necessary, be able to continue part-financing the
applicant states' national contributions.

Such financing should remain at around 10 per cent of the Phare
appropriation, not including participation in the research and development framework programme. The applicant states should be allowed
to take part, as observers and for the points which concern them, in the
management committees responsible for monitoring the programmes to
which they contribute financially, under specific arrangements adapted
to the case in question.

As regards Cyprus, the European Council concluded that accession

> should benefit all communities and help to bring about civil peace and
> reconciliation. The accession negotiations will contribute positively to
> the search for a political solution to the Cyprus problem through the
> talks under the aegis of the United Nations which must continue with a
> view to creating a bi-community, bi-zonal federation. In this context, the
> European Council requests that the willingness of the Government of
> Cyprus to include representatives of the Turkish Cypriot community in
> the accession negotiating delegation be acted upon.

As regards Turkey, the European Council confirmed Turkey's eligibility for accession to the European Union. Turkey will be judged on the basis of the same criteria as the other applicant states. While the political and economic conditions allowing accession negotiations to be envisaged are not satisfied, the European Council considers that it is nevertheless important for a strategy to be drawn up to prepare Turkey for accession by bringing it closer to the European Union in every field.

This strategy should consist of:

- development of the possibilities afforded by the Ankara Agreement;
- intensification of the custom union;
- implementation of financial cooperation;
- approximation of laws and adoption of the Union *acquis*;
- participation, to be decided case by case, in certain programmes and in certain agencies.

In addition, participation in the European Conference will enable the Member States of the European Union and Turkey to step up their dialogue and cooperation in areas of common interest.

The European Council recalled that the strengthening of Turkey's links with the European Union also depends on that country's pursuit of the political and economic reforms on which it has embarked, including the alignment of human rights standards and practices on those in force in the European Union; respect for and protection of minorities; the establishment of satisfactory and stable relations between Greece and Turkey; the settlement of disputes, in particular by legal process, including the International Court of Justice; and support for negotiations under the aegis of the UN on a political settlement in Cyprus on the basis of the relevant UN Security Council resolutions.

On the other elements of Agenda 2000 the European Council

welcomed the Commission's proposals as an appropriate working basis for further negotiations for an agreement on the Union's policies and the financial framework.

The European Council's conclusions were welcomed by the Member States and by nearly all candidate states, with the exception of Turkey. The European Council President, Jean-Claude Juncker, described the outcome as 'monumental' whilst Commission President Santer stated that it 'had opened the path to the peaceful unification of our continent'. Hungarian Prime Minister Gyula Horn called the conclusions 'a historic decision'. Polish Premier Jerzy Buzek expressed his 'deep satisfaction' with the results, and Latvian Prime Minister Guntars Krasts, speaking for the 'pre-ins', described the outcome as 'a formula that we fully accept'.

Turkey, however, was sharply critical of the European Council conclusions, describing them in a statement by Prime Minister Yilmez as 'unacceptable'. He disputed that Turkey had been treated fairly and rejected the proposal that Turkey should participate in the European Conference. The statement did not, however, maintain previous threats to break the customs union or withdraw the Turkish application for EU membership. A separate foreign ministry statement also criticized the decision to open accession negotiations with Cyprus, warning that this was incompatible with the international status of the island.

8 |

The Implications of Enlargement

The possible implications of enlargement have been the subject of considerable study by the Commission, by the Member States and by academics. The Commission produced an interim report for the European Council in Madrid in December 1995 which drew a favourable balance concerning the likely impact of enlargement.[1] It followed this up with a more detailed Impact Study which was published as part of Agenda 2000 (see below).

Member States were concerned at the likely cost of enlargement, particularly its impact on the big spending policies such as agriculture and the structural funds, whilst some also expressed concern at the institutional problems. The IGC had been asked to consider the institutional aspects of enlargement and make proposals for changes to ensure the continued efficiency of the Union's decision-making structures and a fair balance between large and small Member States following enlargement. But the protocol on the institutions, attached to the Amsterdam Treaty, was rather vague, and consisted of just two articles.

Article 1

At the date of entry into force of the first enlargement of the Union, notwithstanding Article 157(1) of the Treaty establishing the European Community, Article 9(1) of the Treaty establishing the European Coal and Steel Community and Article 126(1) of the Treaty establishing the European Atomic Energy Community, the Commission shall comprise one national of each of the Member States, provided that, by that date, the weighting of the votes in the Council has been modified, whether by reweighting of the votes or by dual majority, in a manner acceptable to all Member States, taking into account all relevant elements, notably

1.   Interim report from the Commission to the European Council on the Effects on the Policies of the European Union of Enlargement to the Associated Countries of Central and Eastern Europe SEC (95) 606.

compensating those Member States which give up the possibility of nominating a second member of the Commission.

Article 2

At least one year before the membership of the European Union exceeds twenty, a conference of representatives of the governments of the Member States shall be convened in order to carry out a comprehensive review of the provisions of the Treaties on the composition and functioning of the institutions.

Three Member States (Belgium, France and Italy) issued a declaration at the time of signing the Amsterdam Treaty making clear that their approval of future enlargement would depend on progress in reforming the institutions. Some of the CEECs expressed concern that this sensitive issue might act as a brake on enlargement.

Economic Impact

On balance, enlargement should be economically beneficial for the Union because it is likely to lead to better performances (economies of scale, higher growth and investment, more technological innovation, stronger global corporate players) than those achieved at present by the existing EU and applicant states. From an EU-wide perspective, the greater heterogeneity in production costs within the Union could become a source of competitive advantage. There is, however, a risk that unaddressed adjustment strains could weaken the overall economic situation of the EU.

The increased size of the internal market combined with the relatively higher growth of the CEECs (productivity gains over the medium term in the applicant countries will be higher than in the EC-15 because of a catching-up effect) and the legal and political security brought by membership should make an enlarged Union more attractive for non-EU foreign investment. New Member States should continue to be an attractive production base for many labour-intensive industries, because of a favourable mix of low labour costs, skilled labour force, EU standards and free access to the world's largest integrated market. This should help to attract non-EU investors who want to be present in the EU market but need low-cost production bases.

Given the experience of past enlargements, as well as the single market programme, the enlarged Union will probably attract larger volumes of direct and portfolio investments. In fact, it will probably experience a deterioration of its global current account for some years because investment in the new members will grow faster than savings, and therefore will have to rely more on non-EU funds. This need not be worrying, provided that profitability of new investment is sufficiently high and that a larger share of funds takes the form of long-term investment (e.g. FDI), to ensure low volatility of capital inflows.

Although the applicant countries trade mostly with existing EU members, the enlarged EU will probably continue to be outward-looking and open to the challenges of international economic competition. This is because most of these countries are small economies that will increasingly rely on trade. Enlargement will lead to a significant reduction in the applicants' external tariffs, which should increase the potential for trade. The applicant countries also have a history of important economic links with regions (e.g. the former Soviet Union) where the countries of EU-15 were not very present. Re-establishing these links when demand picks up could become a source of growth and competitive advantage for the Union.

As the proportion of intra-EU trade rises in total EU trade, however, there is a risk that an enlarged EU might also become more inward-looking. Actions required to address the economic problems of the new members and efforts by EU companies to establish their presence in these markets might have a detrimental effect on trade with, and investment in, other fast-growing markets. Furthermore, the growth of demand from the new members might not be in the fastest-growing sectors at the world level, which may have an adverse impact on the competitivity of the EU.

Although the new applicants are not likely to adopt the single currency on accession—there is probably a need for them to retain macroeconomic flexibility, in particular on exchange rate management—they will have to join at a later stage. Enlargement should have an immediate impact, however, on the prospects of the Euro becoming a strong alternative to the dollar, since many of the applicants will want to hold a large share of their reserves in Euros and to invoice in Euros.

An enlarged Union will become even more dependent on imported sources of supplies, and especially on imported oil and gas. Although there are large coal resources in some of the applicant countries (e.g. Poland), most of them have very limited resources of oil and gas and are currently net energy importers. This dependency will increase as the structure of their energy demand is forecast to change. Indeed, demand for coal is likely to fall in the coming years as these economies shift to cleaner and more efficient energy-combustion processes. At the same time, demand for oil and gas will increase significantly in the coming years, driven by transportation and heating needs. Energy from other sources such as nuclear supplies (which may face considerable opposition in the region), renewable energies and hydroelectricity will be insufficient to meet increasing demand.

As a result, dependency on external suppliers of oil and gas will increase. In practice, this means that the enlarged Union will become rather more dependent on supplies coming from Russia (especially for gas), Caucasian and Central Asian countries (mostly for oil) and the Middle East (oil). Increasing dependency on these countries' supplies could have a number of consequences for the enlarged Union's external relations with these regions. In particular, the enlarged Union will have an enhanced interest in promoting stability in the Caucasus region because of the existence of many pipelines linking the crucial Central Asian and Caspian Sea oil and gas fields with ports on the Black Sea. The enlarged EU will have a clear interest to ensure that these resources can be developed and shipped to EU markets. This will increase the need to promote political stability in Central Asia. Increased dependence on Russia (particularly for gas) means that the EU will also have an increased interest to promote political and economic stability in the country.

The enlarged Union will have many problems to resolve on the environmental front as it seeks to mitigate the damage done in the CEECs during decades of Communist neglect. A significant number of Soviet-style reactors (e.g. in Bulgaria, Lithuania) will be located within an enlarged Union whilst the EU's external frontiers will border areas of concern (e.g. Chernobyl). Public opinion in an enlarged EU may also demand higher standards concerning the safety of nuclear reactors and more generally in environmental issues. This could affect EU attitudes in international fora, and possibly lead to friction with external partners.

An enlarged Union will need to tackle many problems in the area of justice and home affairs. It will have extended external frontiers bordering areas of instability, as well as an extended area in which the cooperation in the field of justice and home affairs will be applied where new problems could arise. Issues such as illegal migration, the management of asylum and immigration policies and the fight against organized crime and drug trafficking will increase in importance and acquire new dimensions. To be effective intensified cooperation in this field within the Union will require parallel action to improve co-operation with key neighbours, notably Russia and other NIS countries, Turkey, the Balkans and North Africa. A major issue which will require careful handling will be the extent to which intra-EU pressure for effective control of the external border can be reconciled with economic and other pressures for facilitating transit for legitimate travellers and goods to and from neighbouring countries.

The External Implications

Enlargement of the Union should increase the weight and influence of the EU in international affairs, bring the Union into more direct contact with neighbours, with whom the EU will have new or extended borders, including Russia, Ukraine and Turkey, and reshape the geopolitical map of Europe. This will have profound implications for European security. In addition, an enlarged EU, with a population of over 450 million, will be an economic giant and the largest trading group in the world. The increased weight and influence in external relations that should accrue to an enlarged EU will be dependent, however, on the further development of internal policies, notably the successful introduction of EMU, as well as Member States demonstrating the necessary political will to ensure the efficient functioning of the new arrangements for CFSP, and the Union developing a coherent approach to its external relations.

The EU's partners, particularly the US, will expect an enlarged EU to take on greater responsibility for its own security, as well as playing a greater role in dealing with global and regional security issues. But this increased international role will depend on the EU developing a credible, coherent and efficient external policy, notably fulfilling expectations with regard to the CFSP. Enlargement, however, is unlikely to facilitate the functioning of the CFSP, as the accession of several new Member States will increase the heterogeneity of interests and perceptions on foreign and security policy and could easily complicate the decision-making process. Enlargement could well trigger a new round of membership applications, including a revival of the Swiss and Norwegian applications.

Enlargement will in principle enhance the EU's security by promoting stability and eliminating 'grey zones' in the region. An assessment of the more detailed implications of enlargement for European security, however, is extremely difficult given the number of imponderables, of which the speed and extent of NATO enlargement, the prospects for a credible European Security and Defence Identity (ESDI), and internal developments in Russia are amongst the most important. Although the OSCE is likely to gain an enhanced role, it seems clear that the EU and NATO will remain the two dominant organizations in Europe. But the different speeds of the enlargement processes could have security implications, particularly for those countries not figuring in either the NATO or EU fast tracks, and create complications for the development of ESDI. It will be important that the EU (and WEU/NATO) utilize every possibility to ensure that there are no new dividing lines in Europe. NATO's commitment to proceed in successive enlargement waves is also likely to cause continuing problems with Russia, regardless of the nature of the proposed charter between NATO and Russia. The enlargement of NATO may also lead to new membership applications, including those from EU Member States not in NATO such as Austria and Finland.

There are unlikely to be any radical changes in the international institutional system as a result of enlargement. It is reasonable to expect, however, that the wider the membership of the Union, the more there will be pressure for changes to be made in the representation, particularly the voting rights, of the Union and the Member States in international organizations. But it is the deepening of the integration process rather than the widening of the Union that will cause the most important changes in EU participation in international organizations. The establishment of EMU, in particular, will have important implications for European representation in the international financial institutions and possibly for other fora such as the G7. The position of the Union will be stronger in many international economic institutions, including the WTO where the EU speaks with one voice on trade matters. It is less true in the IMF, where despite a larger share of voting power (almost a third of total votes), it does not yet speak with one voice. The enlarged Union will thus be able to defend and promote its interests to the extent that it develops the political willingness to speak with one voice. This is not a new issue but it is made more important by enlargement because there is a risk that the growing heterogeneity of

the EU will translate into divergent interests and a confused representation of the Union in international bodies. What may become more
pressing as a result of enlargement is the need for effective coordination among Member States in international fora, irrespective of the
extent of Union competence. Even in areas of Community competence,
the increased diversity of views to be expected as new members accede
to the Union could be a problem. This may well slow down further or
even paralyse the decision-making process, with consequent negative
implications for the Union in international negotiations.

Relations with Russia, Ukraine and the NIS
The most important of the geopolitical issues raised by EU enlargement
is the impact it will have on Russia, as well as the closely linked implications for Ukraine, Belarus and other Newly Independent States (NIS,
being the former republics of the Soviet Union, excepting the Baltic
states). An enlarged EU will contain Member States which were formerly part of the Soviet Union (the Baltic states) and others which were
formerly in a military alliance and economic bloc with the Soviet
Union. An enlarged EU will also surround the 'oblast' of Kaliningrad
which is part of Russia, and it will contain several hundred thousand
Russians, living mainly in Estonia and Latvia. Relations between the
candidate countries and Russia are generally good. The lack of interest,
on both sides, in developing these relations during the years immediately following the disintegration of the former Soviet Union has been
replaced by a mutual desire to develop relations on a pragmatic footing.
But it will be important for the enlarged EU to deepen considerably its
relationship with Russia and to monitor carefully the situation of the
Russian minorities in new Member States in order to ensure that they
do not become a stumbling block to better relations.

In general, neither Russia nor any other NIS has voiced any objection
to EU enlargement, although there have been some expressions of concern about possible trade consequences. Russian leaders have recognized that a zone of peace, stability and prosperity in Central and
Eastern Europe will be of benefit also to Russia. Enlargement could,
however, result in increased demands for accession from Ukraine,
Moldova and possibly other NIS. It will be important for the Union to
increase significantly its economic, financial and technical assistance to
these countries. Apart from Russia, Ukraine will be the most important
neighbouring state in Europe, with borders to four new EU Member

States (Poland, Hungary, Slovakia, Romania) who will seek to ensure that EU–Ukrainian relations are not neglected. Belarus will also become more important for the EU as it will border three new Member States (Latvia, Lithuania, Poland). The range of issues associated with external frontiers of the Union will impact particularly on Ukraine, Belarus and Russia. It will be in the interest of an enlarged EU to develop closer links with individual NIS, and to promote political and economic stability.

The EU has a major long-term interest in a stable, prosperous Russia with which it can trade in an increasing number of areas. Trade relations between the applicant states and Russia declined substantially after the collapse of Communism but they have recovered to some extent and there is considerable scope for future growth. The EU's trade with Russia is likely to increase gradually and it will be important to diversify the export structure away from the current situation whereby Russia provides natural resources in return for manufactured and consumer goods. Negotiations for a free trade area between the EU and Russia are envisaged in the Partnership and Cooperation Agreement (PCA), which provides a comprehensive framework to develop relations in numerous fields ranging from foreign and security policy to financial and technical assistance, transport and energy. But the provisions of the PCA may have to be complemented further as a result of the enlarged EU developing a deeper relationship with Russia. This relationship will cover not only political, security, economic and trade issues, but also issues related to the third pillar. It will be important to engage Russia in a constructive dialogue and where possible in joint actions to combat many of the new threats affecting European security.

Transatlantic Relations
The implications of enlargement for transatlantic relations are likely to be diverse and difficult to predict with any certainty. Security and economic issues are likely to remain the twin driving forces of the relationship. As the CEECs join the EU, the corresponding ethnic lobbies in the US could play an important role in certain policy areas. The US has always been a strong supporter of EU enlargement, and would like to see as large a membership as possible (including Turkey). The very fact of EU enlargement is thus likely to be a positive factor for transatlantic relations. The US will certainly wish an enlarged EU to take on more responsibilities for its own security, and for regional and global

security, whilst at the same time remaining under the 'leadership' of Washington. The US will continue to view (an enlarged) NATO as its prime vehicle for influence in Europe, and seek to use NATO to support its own bilateral relationships with Russia and Ukraine. While the EU and the US are likely to maintain the same core interests in terms of support for democracy in Russia and stability in the Balkans, North Africa and the NIS, there could well be a weakening of transatlantic ties unless the US is persuaded that the EU is carrying its fair share of the burden. The extent to which the EU develops a coherent and credible CFSP will largely determine how it is viewed by the US. At the same time, a more assertive EU on the international stage could lead to new sources of friction and possibly rivalry in the transatlantic relationship.

On the economic front, an enlarged and more competitive EU could challenge the US for a larger share of world markets. Enlargement could also heighten disagreements on some sectors (e.g. steel, agriculture) where the EU's competitiveness in world (and US) markets could be significantly increased. Similarly, although on a narrower focus, enlargement may increase the risk of anti-dumping actions against the EU with, again, a potentially negative impact on trade and broader relations. Although continuing substantial trade and investment ties between the EU and the US are likely to ensure that the transatlantic relationship remains the most important global relationship in the world, relatively minor trade disagreements could have important political ramifications and alter the environment in which the relationship takes place. The economic relationship is one where the short- to medium-term interests of the Union and the US are likely to diverge, competing for shares of third country markets (especially the big emerging markets), use of multilateral versus unilateral trade policy, differing positions within and concerning the WTO. There are areas, particularly in the economic/financial domain, where the increased weight of the EU might alter the relative position of the EU and the US.

It is likely that enlargement will reinforce the transatlantic relationship in a number of other areas of mutual concern such as drugs, crime, health and the environment. In the case of drugs, concerns about transit through the CEECs may be alleviated as they become members of the Union and integrated fully within third pillar activities.

The Balkans

The future political and economic development of the Balkans is equally difficult to predict but EU enlargement will certainly increase rather than diminish the importance of the Balkans to the Union because of its geographical position in relation to an enlarged EU. Enlargement should contribute to increased stability in the region as the new Member States will press for an intensification of relations between the EU and the Balkans. Enlargement could also trigger new accession demands from some countries in the region who in the next decade might have negotiated Europe Agreements. Divergent courses between members and non-members in the Balkans, by which the latter would be marginalized in a 'grey zone' of conflicts, instability and economic underdevelopment, could pose a major threat to security. The EU will thus have to pay increased attention to the Balkans to counter these risks and ensure the closest possible relations with the states in the region according to their political and economic development, and maintaining the conditionality already agreed as a basis for policy. Intensified regional cooperation, including support for the Black Sea Economic Cooperation (BSEC), will be particularly important in this regard.

The Developing Countries

It is important that an enlarged EU should maintain its political, economic, technical and financial support for the developing countries, in order that its broad humanitarian, economic (open and expanding markets) and political (regional stability) objectives can be met. The immediate challenge will be to deal with concern on the part of the developing countries about the EU's preoccupation with internal issues and the flow of financial resources to the new members and countries in the immediate neighbourhood. This may not prove to be easy. On the one hand enlargement and the resulting impetus which this will give to economic growth will increase the resources potentially available for external assistance. On the other hand, enlargement will change the balance of power within the EU: new members which are relatively poor and do not have the colonial history of many existing members may give a low priority to development cooperation.

The new Member States will have production structures similar to those of many middle-income developing countries, notably in Asia and Latin America. This may make it more difficult to agree further regional trading initiatives, an increasingly important aspect of the EU's policy towards developing countries. Despite the potential problems, it will be important that an enlarged EU continues to maintain an open trade policy. This applies to bilateral relations, to regional trading agreements and, multilaterally, in the WTO, where the EU must play a leading role and continue to be supportive of the developing countries.

Regional Cooperation

The importance of regional cooperation for an enlarged Union will remain undiminished. Such cooperation promotes stability at the external borders of the Union and is an important aspect of preparing future candidates for accession. The EU has an interest in continuing to promote regional cooperation amongst those countries (and regions) which will not join the EU at an early date. The Barents Sea initiative will deserve continuing EU support as it engages Russia (and other non-Member States) in important cross-border projects. The Baltic Sea Cooperation Council should receive a new impetus as a result of new Member States' participation. It remains to be seen whether and under which format the Central European Initiative (CEI) will continue in existence, but its importance in bringing together Member and non-Member States should give it an additional importance. Enlargement of the Union to the south will focus increased attention on the Balkan and Black Sea regions. Both regions are likely to gain in importance for the Union as a result of enlargement and the EU will wish to develop further its relations with the states of both regions as well as the regional organizations, including the Black Sea Economic Cooperation group. In short the EU should maintain and augment its support for regional cooperation whilst recognizing that the diversity of schemes and Member States will require a diversified approach.

EU enlargement will thus have significant international implications, notably for the EU's most important neighbours and partners. In the first instance, the EU will need to pay more attention to Russia, Ukraine and Turkey, the three major non-EU actors on the European continent, plus the Mediterranean region. Enlargement should enhance the EU's ability to develop a sound and more intense relationship with those countries most directly affected by enlargement. Secondly, enlargement should lead to an intensification of relations with the US, but there is also the potential for disputes to arise as a result of enlargement.

Thirdly, enlargement should reinforce the EU as an international economic actor, and not just in the trade dimension. It should also lead to greater FDI flows into the EU, as a result of an enlarged and more dynamic internal market. Fourthly, enlargement should lead to greater EU influence on the world stage, providing its internal policies, including EMU, continue in a satisfactory manner, and it develops the capacity to speak and act with one voice.

Impact Study

As part of the Agenda 2000 report (COM (97)2000 Vol II) the Commission produced an Impact Study on the effects on the Union's policies of enlargement to the CEECs. The following extract is the summary of the Impact Study, pp. 97-107.

Overall Economic Impact

Economic benefits from enlargement are expected to result from the expansion of the Single Market, from the overall integration process, as well as from the strengthening of the Union's position in global markets. The Union's human potential will be considerably enriched, not least in qualified and highly qualified labour. Acceding countries have significant natural resources (agricultural land, some minerals, biodiversity, etc.). Their geographic position will be an asset with respect to transport, energy transit and communications. The integration of these countries into the Union will be a powerful stimulus to their economic development. Major investments related to the radical modernization of the acceding countries' economies and their catching up with EU living standards will boost demand across the Union and strengthen competitiveness.

At the same time, substantial sectoral and regional adjustment pressure will result from the enlargement process, although implementation of the Europe Agreements will have integrated EU and candidate country markets considerably by the time of accession. Sensitive areas for the Union as a whole could include the labour market (though alarmist forecasts would not seem justified), certain industries, especially in labour-intensive and other traditional sectors, some areas of transport, etc. The regional distribution of costs and benefits from enlargement is difficult to assess, but inordinate pessimism with regard to the impact on the less developed regions in the current Member States does not seem justified.

In acceding countries, strains resulting from increased competitive pressure could initially be more widespread and could affect large sectors of industry, including small and medium-sized enterprises (SME's), agriculture and fisheries, services, the audiovisual sector. They could also affect the financial system and the balance of payments. Were such problems not to be addressed by appropriate measures, especially before accession, their impact on new Member States could be quite serious, and would thus also burden Community policies. Moreover, there would be spill-over risks to the rest of the Union (e.g. in the labour market), though in many areas (e.g. the financial system) such risks would be limited by the relatively small size of acceding country economies.

The economic gains to be reaped from enlargement will depend primarily on the conditions in which the Single Market is enlarged, which in turn depend on the progress which the associated countries are able to make between now and accession in aligning their laws and practices with those of the EU. Economic gains will also depend on the adequacy of transport, telecommunication and energy infrastructures and networks in acceding countries, which are necessary to support the increased trade and economic activity resulting from integration.

Structural Policies

The new enlargement concerns a group of countries in a clearly unfavourable socio-economic situation, as compared to that of existing Member States. Under present rules all regions of candidate countries would be eligible for Objective 1 support. Considering the legacies of the past, rapid transition towards the market, and the scale of the necessary effort for participating in the Single Market, success of integration and the capacity of economic operators to reap its benefits will largely depend on the intensity of structural actions that can be directed to the acceding countries. Such actions should primarily aim at reducing the distance of new members to the Community average, but also at reducing their increasing internal disparities.

Enlargement will not substantially alleviate the problems of regions and population groups eligible for structural aids in present Member States (in particular in Objective 1 regions); it could also generate some adjustment pressure. Hence Community interventions to such regions and groups will be continued, as they play a decisive role in structural development and in the global catching up within the EU-15. Changes will be made, to take account of progress accomplished in some regions in terms of real convergence and of the need of concentration of the Community effort. Changes are advisable also for increasing efficiency, control and simplification within the framework of budgetary discipline which implies a levelling off in relative terms of the cohesion effort after 1999. These principles should be applied both to present and to acceding Member States.

Already now, a gradual two stage preaccession strategy must start being implemented (1997–1999, 2000-accession dates), with Community support, to prepare candidate countries for the adoption of the *acquis* in this field. On accession, all dispositions in force concerning structural policies must be applied to the new members, including technical adjustments that would prove necessary and would justify the existence of a specific phase. Financial amounts to be allocated to new members will be determined so as to take into account absorptive capacities, the necessary efficiency of structural spending, as well as a progressive increase of per capita support.

In an enlarged EU territory, economic and social cohesion should be taken into account more than ever in the formulation and implementation of every Community policy.

Agriculture

Enlargement will greatly increase the agricultural potential of the Union, while the market for European primary products and processed food will increase by more than 100 million consumers. Trade in these products between existing and acceding members will be fully liberalized. These developments should improve economic welfare in the Union as a whole. At the same time, adjustment strains from exposure of the candidate countries to competition could be considerable, not least in terms of a significant shedding of surplus labour. To a lesser extent, problems could also arise for some products in the present Member States.

Extension of the Common Agricultural Policy (CAP) in its present form to the acceding countries would create difficulties. Given existing price gaps between candidate countries and generally substantially higher CAP prices, and despite prospects for some narrowing of these gaps by the dates of accession, even gradual introduction of CAP prices would tend to stimulate surplus production, in particular in the livestock sector, thus adding to projected surpluses. World Trade Organization (WTO) constraints on subsidized exports would prevent the enlarged Union to sell its surpluses on third markets. Extension of the CAP would also entail an important budgetary charge, estimated at around 11 billion ECU per year, direct payments to farmers representing close to 2/3 of this sum.

Substantial rises in agricultural prices and important direct transfers to farmers would have a negative economic and social impact on acceding countries. Moreover, direct payments, conceived as compensation for price reductions, would not be justified for farmers in acceding countries who would face price rises instead.

In view of the growing market imbalances foreseen for the EU after 2000 (even without enlargement), further adjustments in the current support policies would probably be needed. A reorientation of the CAP with less focus on price support and more on direct income support as well as on rural development and environmental policy was already suggested in the Agricultural Strategy Paper of 1995. This would help to reduce the price gap and would provide support for the structural adjustment process of acceding countries. In the latter context, in place of direct payments to farmers, a significant amount of the money could be used, at least during a transitional period, for structural reforms and rural development in these countries.

Adequate implementation and enforcement of the Community *acquis* in the candidate countries is essential for the protection of plant, animal and public health in an enlarged Union as a whole. It must be accomplished before free movement of agricultural products without border control can be established. The implementation of these measures will require substantial investment and time.

Internal Market and Economic and Monetary Union

Internal Market. The impact of enlargement on the functioning of the Internal Market will largely depend on the extent of economic benefits which will result from enlargement, but also on the management of sectoral and regional strains resulting from the adjustment process. Market distortions and prejudice to EU consumers could result from possible inadequate implementation of the Internal Market *acquis*. Sensitive areas in this respect include implementation of the *acquis* regulating free movement of goods, the protection of health, environment and consumers, indirect taxation, adequate management of the external borders, implementation of safety requirements and state aids. The capacity of acceding countries' administrations to manage the Community *acquis* will be a key element. The more this capacity is achieved before accession, the fewer problems will arise after it. If important problems were to remain after accession, protectionist political pressure could develop in both present and acceding Member States and could endanger the functioning of the Internal Market as a whole.

Economic and Monetary Union. Enlargement will take place during stage three of Economic and Monetary Union. This creates a major challenge for acceding members, since they will have to implement the *acquis communautaire* in this area, at least as non-participant countries if, as it can be expected, most or all of them will not initially participate in EMU. It will thus be important for acceding countries to undertake the necessary reforms permitting them to stabilize their economies in the long-run, as well as to avoid disruptive movements in nominal exchange rates and misalignments that could threaten the proper operation of the Single Market. Enlargement could shift the institutional balance between EMU participants and non-participants, but the impact on the dynamics of EMU is likely to be limited. Most candidate countries have adopted a positive approach towards EMU.

Social Policy. Social policy in an enlarged Union will have to address the acute social problems of acceding countries, including unemployment and public health issues, as well as problems resulting from the adjustment process in both old and new Member States. Important investment in human resources will be necessary and Community social policy and its funding will be burdened accordingly. Adaptation of acceding countries to the Community social *acquis* and the European social model could be adversely affected by the large number of citizens having a standard of living far below the EU average, by insufficiently developed vocational training networks, by systems of industrial relations still in transition and in need of improvement, and by inefficient public administrations. In some areas, for instance in health and safety at work, adaptation of acceding countries to the Community *acquis*, while benefiting the well-being of workers and enhancing productivity, will require serious and sometimes costly efforts. However, too slow or inadequate adaptation could have adverse effects on competition and could complicate further development of Community policies. On the other hand, enlargement will highlight the importance of social cohesion in the objectives of the Treaties and should thus enhance the role of social policy.

Environment. Enlargement to new members which face severe environmental problems will present a considerable challenge for Community policy in this field. The gap between acceding and present members in the levels of environmental protection will gradually have to be bridged, for environmental and for economic reasons, and this will necessitate massive investment in the acceding countries, mainly in the public utility sectors for water, energy and waste, but also by enterprises. A major effort will also be needed in developing the administrative structures for implementation and enforcement of EU environmental law. EU financial assistance, both before and after accession, should contribute to keep adaptation within reasonable time-limits. A risk that Community environmental policy will be diverted away from global issues, and that membership by countries enjoying lower standards will hamper its further development will have to be addressed. At the same time, EU responsibility for problems having cross-border effects and already largely affecting European citizens will increase. In this sense, enlargement does not *create* problems, but will rather highlight them and improve the framework for their solution. Enlargement is likely to further strengthen a more flexible approach to EU environmental regulation with a stronger emphasis on implementation and enforcement.

Consumers. On the whole, enlargement should benefit EU consumers by increasing their choices and by improving the level of protection in acceding countries. However, Community consumer policy will have to be strengthened in order to take account of increased disparities resulting from enlargement. Eventual inadequacy of control structures and business ethics could result in the creation of 'weak links' which would adversely affect the functioning of the enlarged Internal Market.

Sectoral Policies

Transport. Expansion of the Single Market through enlargement should benefit the transport sector as well. However, important financial resources, partly from EU funds, will be needed for the development of transport networks, for adaptation of acceding countries and their transport fleets to Community social, safety and other technical requirements, as well as for encouraging a favourable modal development in line with the orientations of the Common Transport Policy. Possible inadequate preparation of candidate countries before accession could adversely affect competition within the Internal Market, and would increase protectionist political pressure which is also likely to result from adjustment strains in the transport sector ...

Energy. Enlargement would not seem to create major problems for the Union and its policies in the energy sector, while it will bring accompanying benefits with respect to stability of energy supplies, research, and energy efficiency on a continental scale. These benefits should have a positive impact on security and peace in the region. Important investments will be necessary to ensure upgrading and adaptation to the EU *acquis*, and such investment will generate demand from related EU industries. However, lack of sufficient funds constitutes in certain countries a bottleneck, and, as in other sectors, preparation during the preaccession period will be a critical factor. EU energy policy would have to take account of the realities of an enlarged Union, such as an increased dependency on Russia, or the economic and social consequences of mine restructuring in acceding countries. Achievement of its objectives (e.g. completion of the internal energy market) could prove more difficult in an enlarged Union. However, in several areas (including nuclear safety and environmental norms) problems for the Union and its policies would be even more serious without the effort related to accession. In some candidate countries, *nuclear safety* is a problem with a broader regional and European significance, causing serious concern throughout the continent. The solution of this problem in accordance with the Community *acquis* and by promoting a 'nuclear safety culture' is thus a crucial and urgent task.

Industry. Enlargement should on the whole benefit Community industry, as a result of the expected increase in economic activity and improved resource allocation. However, significant adjustment strains can be expected in both acceding and present members. During an initial period, low-cost production will be a comparative advantage of acceding countries...

Telecommunications. No major problems are expected from enlargement for Community telecommunications policy, while the market for the telecommunications sector will expand. A considerable shortfall in investment is likely to generate demand for Community funding...

Small and Medium-sized Enterprises. Enlargement will expose SME's in acceding countries to considerable competitive pressure. Hence EU policies will have to focus on supporting their adjustment...

Fisheries. No serious problems should arise from enlargement for the Common Fisheries Policy (CFP). The Union's fishery resources will not increase significantly. Fishing sectors in some coastal regions of acceding countries, already in deep crisis due to problems of overcapacity and obsolescence, will have to be restructured, with possible sensitive social repercussions which will have to be addressed. Cooperation already under way in the Baltic will facilitate integration, but Community policies will also have to tackle problems related to fisheries in the Black Sea. The capacity of some candidate countries to implement the *acquis* should, nevertheless, be closely monitored.

Justice and Home Affairs

The expansion of the Union will provide both a challenge and an opportunity to tackle common transnational problems in the fields of migration and asylum, police and customs cooperation and judicial cooperation affecting the current EU and the countries of Central and Eastern Europe. Just as any weaknesses in the defences of the applicant countries in these areas will represent a threat to the existing EU Member States, so also strong Justice and Home Affairs (JHA) performance in candidate countries will contribute positively to security and freedom of citizens in the present EU. It is also in the general interest to ensure that Justice and Home Affairs measures are applied according to common and high standards throughout the enlarged Union and that each acceding state is able to meet adequately EU requirements. Hence the importance of associating candidate countries to these measures as much as possible in advance of accession, and to provide the necessary technical assistance. The process is already under way. The more it is strengthened, the less spill-over of crime and fraud into the Union will occur and the fewer will be the problems upon accession.

9 |

NATO Enlargement

Since the fall of the Berlin Wall and the end of the Cold War, NATO has also transformed itself and prepared for enlargement. Despite widespread scepticism about NATO's *raison d'être* after the disappearance of the Soviet threat, the transformation of the Alliance has been an important part of the overall process of building a new European security architecture.

The Washington Treaty was signed on 4 April 1949 as a response to the growing Soviet threat in Europe. Its main aim was 'to deter and defend against any aggression against the territory of any NATO member state'. It further provided for the military integration of the armed forces of Member States in a unified command structure. The founding members were the US, the UK, France, Canada, Italy, Belgium, the Netherlands, Luxembourg, Norway, Iceland and Denmark. Greece and Turkey joined in 1952, the Federal Republic of Germany in 1955 and Spain in 1982.

NATO was highly valued by its Member States during the Cold War, successfully carrying out its deterrent function, and not having to fire a shot in anger. The first signs of a changed security environment appeared in May 1990 when NATO announced that it no longer considered the Warsaw Pact a threat to the Alliance. At NATO's London Summit in July 1990 the final declaration invited the former adversaries to establish diplomatic liaison offices and to develop military cooperation. The London Declaration also stated the intent to reduce and restructure NATO forces, to reduce the reliance on forward deployment, and to modify the strategic concept of flexible response.

This move by NATO was important in securing Soviet acceptance of a united Germany within NATO. Initially, Moscow was strongly opposed to East Germany becoming part of NATO following unification. But faced with a united Western front, it eventually agreed during the 4 plus 2 negotiations on the united Germany being a full member of NATO. It did, however, secure some concessions regarding limitations on German and NATO troops and infrastructure in eastern Germany.

At the NATO Summit in Rome in December 1991 NATO agreed to strengthen cooperation between NATO and the former members of the Warsaw Pact. The next major step in the evolution of NATO came at the Brussels Summit in January 1994, when the Partnership for Peace programme (PfP) was offered to all democratic countries in the OSCE. PfP aimed at deepening the bilateral political and military relations between NATO and the participating countries through increased practical cooperation.

The North Atlantic Cooperation Council (NACC) and PfP were partly destined to forestall full NATO membership applications and thus did not satisfy those CEECs keen to join the Alliance. Several CEECs were critical towards the 'Russia first' policy pursued by the Clinton administration since taking office in December 1992, fearing a Russian *droit de regard* over their status in European security. However, by mid-1994 pressure for a more determined approach towards enlargement was mounting. The German Minister of Defence Volker Rühe was a strong advocate of NATO enlargement and contracted a study by the US think tank RAND of the implications of enlargement. The US administration was also beginning to shift due to pressure from ethnic minorities (e.g. the Polish lobby in electorally important Illinois), increased Republican pressure to accept the Visegrad countries as members, and concern after the ultranationalist victory in the December 1993 Russian Duma election.

To mask disagreements in the Alliance it was agreed in December 1994 that NATO would carry out a study on enlargement. After this decision, NATO enlargement was no longer a question of 'if', but rather 'who and when', and the political approach then focused on deepening relations with Russia in parallel with NATO's own enlargement—a dual track policy.

The Enlargement Study was published in September 1995 and to the disappointment of the CEECs it avoided the questions of who and when. Rather it dealt with the more general questions of 'why and how'. The Study stated that NATO's overall approach should focus on a framework of interlocking institutions, that bilateral relations with Russia should be strengthened, and finally it confirmed that NATO would enlarge. Furthermore, the Study stressed that enlargement was not a matter of expanding the sphere of influence or creating new dividing lines in Europe.

It was specified that obtaining membership required full participation on both the political and military level. In order to enjoy the benefits of membership the new members must be able to undertake the responsibilities stated in the Washington Treaty. Finally, it was made explicit that NACC and PfP still had very important roles to play for the countries that would not obtain membership.

Study on Nato Enlargement (Extracts)[1]

A. *Why NATO Will Enlarge/Purposes of Enlargement*

1—With the end of the Cold War, there is a unique opportunity to build an improved security architecture in the whole of the Euro-Atlantic area. The aim of an improved security architecture is to provide increased stability and security for all in the Euro-Atlantic area, without recreating dividing lines. NATO views security as a broad concept embracing political and economic, as well as defence, components. Such a broad concept of security should be the basis for the new security architecture which must be built through a gradual process of integration and cooperation brought about by an interplay of existing multilateral institutions in Europe, such as the EU, WEU and OSCE, each of which would have a role to play in accordance with its respective responsibilities and purposes in implementing this broad security concept. In this process, which is already well under way, the Alliance has played and will play a strong, active and essential role as one of the cornerstones of stability and security in Europe. NATO remains a purely defensive Alliance whose fundamental purpose is to preserve peace in the Euro-Atlantic area and to provide security for its members.

2—When NATO invites other European countries to become Allies...this will be a further step towards the Alliance's basic goal of enhancing security and stability throughout the Euro-Atlantic area, within the context of a broad European security architecture. NATO enlargement will extend to new members the benefits of common defence and integration into European and Euro-Atlantic institutions. The benefits of common defence and such integration are important to protecting the further democratic development of new members... Meeting NATO's fundamental security goals and supporting the integration of new members into European and Euro-Atlantic institutions are thus complementary goals of the enlargement process, consistent with the Alliance's strategic concept.

---

1.   The full study on NATO Enlargement, published on 5 September 1995, may be found on the NATO web site (see Bibliography).

3—Therefore, enlargement will contribute to enhanced stability and security for all countries in the Euro-Atlantic area by:

- Encouraging and supporting democratic reforms, including civilian and democratic control over the military;
- Fostering in new members of the Alliance the patterns and habits of cooperation, consultation and consensus building which characterize relations among current Allies;
- Promoting good-neighbourly relations, which would benefit all countries in the Euro-Atlantic area, both members and non-members of NATO;
- Emphasizing common defence and extending its benefits and increasing transparency in defence planning and military budgets, thereby reducing the likelihood of instability that might be engendered by an exclusively national approach to defence policies;
- Reinforcing the tendency toward integration and cooperation in Europe based on shared democratic values and thereby curbing the countervailing tendency towards disintegration along ethnic and territorial lines;
- Strengthening the Alliance's ability to contribute to European and international security, including through peacekeeping activities under the responsibility of the OSCE and peacekeeping operations under the authority of the UN Security Council as well as other new missions;
- Strengthening and broadening the Trans-Atlantic partnership.

B. *Principles of Enlargement*

4—Enlargement of the Alliance will be through accession of new Member States to the Washington Treaty. Enlargement should:

- Accord with, and help to promote, the purposes and principles of the Charter of the United Nations, and the safeguarding of the freedom, common heritage and civilization of all Alliance members and their people, founded on the principles of democracy, individual liberty and the rule of law. New members will need to conform to these basic principles;
- Accord strictly with Article 10 of the Washington Treaty which states that 'the parties may, by unanimous agreement, invite any other European state in a position to further the principles of this Treaty and to contribute to the security of the North Atlantic area to accede to this Treaty...';
- Be on the basis that new members will enjoy all the rights and assume all obligations of membership under the Washington Treaty; and accept and conform with the principles, policies and procedures adopted by all members of the Alliance at the time that new members join;

- Strengthen the Alliance's effectiveness and cohesion; and preserve the Alliance's political and military capability to perform its core functions of common defence as well as to undertake peacekeeping and other new missions;
- Be part of a broad European security architecture based on true cooperation throughout the whole of Europe. It would threaten no-one; and enhance stability and security for all of Europe;
- Take account of the continuing important role of PfP, which will both help prepare interested partners, through their participation in PfP activities, for the benefits and responsibilities of eventual membership and serve as a means to strengthen relations with partner countries which may be unlikely to join the Alliance early or at all. Active participation in the Partnership for Peace will play an important role in the evolutionary process of the enlargement of NATO;
- Complement the enlargement of the European Union, a parallel process which also, for its part, contributes significantly to extending security and stability to the new democracies in the East.

5—New members, at the time that they join, must commit themselves, as all current Allies do on the basis of the Washington Treaty, to:

- unite their efforts for collective defence and for the preservation of peace and security; settle any international disputes in which they may be involved by peaceful means in such a manner that international peace and security and justice are not endangered, and refrain in their international relations from the threat or use of force in any manner inconsistent with the purposes of the United Nations;
- contribute to the development of peaceful and friendly international relations by strengthening their free institutions, by bringing about a better understanding of the principles upon which these institutions are founded, and by promoting conditions of stability and well-being;
- maintain the effectiveness of the Alliance by sharing roles, risks, responsibilities, costs and benefits of assuring common security goals and objectives.

6—States which have ethnic disputes or external territorial disputes, including irredentist claims, or internal jurisdictional disputes must settle those disputes by peaceful means in accordance with OSCE principles. Resolution of such disputes would be a factor in determining whether to invite a state to join the Alliance.

7—Decisions on enlargement will be for NATO itself. Enlargement will occur through a gradual, deliberate, and transparent process, encompassing dialogue with all interested parties. There is no fixed or rigid list of criteria for inviting new Member States to join the Alliance. Enlargement will be decided on a case-by-case basis and some nations may attain membership before others. New members should not be admitted or excluded on the basis of belonging to some group or category. Ultimately, Allies will decide by consensus whether to invite each new member to join according to their judgment of whether doing so will contribute to security and stability in the North Atlantic area at the time such a decision is to be made. NATO enlargement would proceed in accordance with the provisions of the various OSCE documents which confirm the sovereign right of each state to freely seek its own security arrangements, to belong or not to belong to international organizations, including treaties of alliance. No country outside the Alliance should be given a veto or *droit de regard* over the process and decisions.

8—NATO's collective defence arrangements are a concrete expression of Allies' commitment to maintain and develop their individual and collective capacity to resist armed attack. Against the background of existing arrangements for contributing to collective defence, Allies will want to know how possible new members intend to contribute to NATO's collective defence and will explore all aspects of this question in detail through bilateral dialogue prior to accession negotiations.

Russian Reactions

After the dissolution of the Soviet Union and Russian independence on 31 December 1991 the new Russian government and in particular President Yeltsin and Minister of Foreign Affairs Kozyrev pursued a pro-Western foreign policy. The Russian leaders welcomed the transformation of NATO in a more political direction, the focus on institutional interaction, and NATO's reduced capability of posing a military threat.

But Russia was also opposed to NATO's dominant position in European security and preferred the OSCE collective security structure. Many Russians argued that NATO as well as the Warsaw Pact was a product of the Cold War and ultimately ought to be dissolved. Under pressure from nationalists in the Duma, the Yeltsin government began to pursue a more assertive foreign policy. Initially there was a strong scepticism in Moscow towards NACC and PfP as they were viewed as instruments to enhance NATO's influence in the OSCE area. But it soon became obvious to Russia that it would lose influence itself if it did not sign up to PfP. Eventually, in June 1994 it reached agreement on PfP but postponed signing the agreement as a result of the NATO decision to proceed with enlargement.

As was widely expected, strong rhetorical opposition was the immediate Russian reaction when NATO published the Enlargement Study in September 1995. However, from then on the enlargement process was de facto irreversible, and therefore the Russian government gradually moderated its rhetoric in order not to lose face.

Following intense negotiations throughout spring 1997 the NATO–Russia Agreement on Permanent Joint Council (PJC) was signed on 27 May. Under the agreement, the PJC will hold monthly consultations and make joint decisions on areas such as peace-keeping, conflict prevention, defence planning and budgets, arms control, and restructuring of the arms industry. The PJC is intended to increase the transparency of military planning and operations, and strengthen diplomatic and military cooperation.

The signing of the bilateral treaty in May was by no means a coincidence, as it was very important for both NATO and Russia to strengthen their partnership before NATO's formal enlargement decision was to be taken in July. For NATO it was important to seek rapprochement with Russia in order to avoid misperceptions, whereas the Russian government had to be able to claim having safeguarded Russia's strategic position before the enlargement—once again for domestic political purposes.

Founding Act on Mutual Relations, Cooperation and Security between NATO and the Russian Federation (Extracts)[2]

> The North Atlantic Treaty Organization and its Member States, on the one hand, and the Russian Federation, on the other hand, hereinafter referred to as NATO and Russia, based on an enduring political commitment undertaken at the highest political level, will build together a lasting and inclusive peace in the Euro-Atlantic area on the principles of democracy and cooperative security.
>
> NATO and Russia do not consider each other as adversaries. They share the goal of overcoming the vestiges of earlier confrontation and competition and of strengthening mutual trust and cooperation. The present Act reaffirms the determination of NATO and Russia to give concrete substance to their shared commitment to build a stable, peaceful and undivided Europe, whole and free, to the benefit of all its peoples. Making this commitment at the highest political level marks the beginning of a fundamentally new relationship between NATO and Russia. They intend to develop, on the basis of common interest, reciprocity and transparency a strong, stable and enduring partnership.

2.   The full text is available on the NATO web site (see Bibliography).

This Act defines the goals and mechanism of consultation, cooperation, joint decision-making and joint action that will constitute the core of the mutual relations between NATO and Russia...

II. *Mechanism for Consultation and Cooperation, the NATO–Russia Permanent Joint Council*

To carry out the activities and aims provided for by this Act and to develop common approaches to European security and to political problems, NATO and Russia will create the NATO–Russia Permanent Joint Council. The central objective of this Permanent Joint Council will be to build increasing levels of trust, unity of purpose and habits of consultation and cooperation between NATO and Russia, in order to enhance each other's security and that of all nations in the Euro-Atlantic area and diminish the security of none. If disagreements arise, NATO and Russia will endeavour to settle them on the basis of goodwill and mutual respect within the framework of political consultations.

The Permanent Joint Council will provide a mechanism for consultations, coordination and, to the maximum extent possible, where appropriate, for joint decisions and joint action with respect to security issues of common concern.

The consultations will not extend to internal matters of either NATO, NATO Member States or Russia. The shared objective of NATO and Russia is to identify and pursue as many opportunities for joint action as possible. As the relationship develops, they expect that additional opportunities for joint action will emerge.

...NATO and Russia will promptly consult within the Permanent Joint Council in case one of the Council members perceives a threat to its territorial integrity, political independence or security ...

Provisions of this Act do not provide NATO or Russia, in any way, with a right of veto over the actions of the other nor do they infringe upon or restrict the rights of NATO or Russia to independent decision-making and action. They cannot be used as a means to disadvantage the interests of other states.

The Permanent Joint Council will meet at various levels and in different forms, according to the subject matter and the wishes of NATO and Russia. The Permanent Joint Council will meet at the level of Foreign Ministers and at the level of Defence Ministers twice annually, and also monthly at the level of ambassadors/permanent representatives to the North Atlantic Council.

The Permanent Joint Council may also meet, as appropriate, at the level of Heads of State and Government...

Under the auspices of the Permanent Joint Council, military representatives and Chiefs of Staff will also meet; meetings of Chiefs of Staff will take place no less than twice a year, and also monthly at military representatives level. Meetings of military experts may be convened, as appropriate...

To support the work of the Permanent Joint Council, NATO and Russia will establish the necessary administrative structures.

Russia will establish a Mission to NATO headed by a representative at the rank of Ambassador. A senior military representative and his staff will be part of this Mission for the purposes of the military cooperation. NATO retains the possibility of establishing an appropriate presence in Moscow, the modalities of which remain to be determined...

III. *Areas for Consultation and Cooperation*

In building their relationship, NATO and Russia will focus on specific areas of mutual interest. They will consult and strive to cooperate to the broadest possible degree in the following areas:

- issues of common interest related to security and stability in the Euro-Atlantic area or to concrete crises, including the contribution of NATO and Russia to security and stability in this area;
- conflict prevention, including preventive diplomacy, crisis management and conflict resolution taking into account the role and responsibility of the UN and the OSCE and the work of these organizations in these fields;
- joint operations, including peacekeeping operations, on a case-by-case basis, under the authority of the UN Security Council or the responsibility of the OSCE, and if Combined Joint Task Forces (CJTF) are used in such cases, participation in them at an early stage;
- participation of Russia in the Euro-Atlantic Partnership Council and the Partnership for Peace;
- exchange of information and consultation on strategy, defence policy, the military doctrines of NATO and Russia, and budgets and infrastructure development programmes;
- arms control issues;
- nuclear safety issues, across their full spectrum;
- preventing the proliferation of nuclear, biological and chemical weapons, and their delivery means, combating nuclear trafficking and strengthening cooperation in specific arms control areas, including political and defence aspects of proliferation;
- possible cooperation in Theatre Missile Defence;
- enhanced regional air traffic safety, increased air traffic capacity and reciprocal exchanges, as appropriate, to promote confidence through increased measures of transparency and exchanges of information in relation to air defence and related aspects of airspace management/control. This will include exploring possible cooperation on appropriate air defence related matters;

- increasing transparency, predictability and mutual confidence regarding the size and roles of the conventional forces of Member States of NATO and Russia;
- reciprocal exchanges, as appropriate, on nuclear weapons issues, including doctrines and strategy of NATO and Russia;
- coordinating a programme of expanded cooperation between respective military establishments, as further detailed below;
- pursuing possible armaments-related cooperation through association of Russia with NATO's Conference of National Armaments Directors;
- conversion of defence industries;
- developing mutually agreed cooperative projects in defence-related economic, environmental and scientific fields;
- conducting joint initiatives and exercises in civil emergency preparedness and disaster relief;
- combating terrorism and drug trafficking;
- improving public understanding of evolving relations between NATO and Russia, including the establishment of a NATO documentation centre or information office in Moscow.
- Other areas can be added by mutual agreement.

IV. *Political-Military Matters*

NATO and Russia affirm their shared desire to achieve greater stability and security in the Euro-Atlantic area.

The Member States of NATO reiterate that they have no intention, no plan and no reason to deploy nuclear weapons on the territory of new members, nor any need to change any aspect of NATO's nuclear posture or nuclear policy—and do not foresee any future need to do so.

Recognizing the importance of the adaptation of the Treaty on Conventional Armed Forces in Europe (CFE) for the broader context of security in the OSCE area and the work on a Common and Comprehensive Security Model for Europe for the twenty-first Century, the Member States of NATO and Russia will work together in Vienna with the other States Parties to adapt the CFE Treaty to enhance its viability and effectiveness, taking into account Europe's changing security environment and the legitimate security interests of all OSCE participating States.

The Member States of NATO and Russia will strive for greater transparency, predictability and mutual confidence with regard to their armed forces. They will comply fully with their obligations under the Vienna Document 1994 and develop cooperation with the other OSCE participating States, including negotiations in the appropriate format, inter alia within the OSCE to promote confidence and security.

The Member States of NATO and Russia will use and improve existing arms control regimes and confidence-building measures to create security relations based on peaceful cooperation.

NATO and Russia, in order to develop cooperation between their military establishments, will expand political-military consultations and cooperation through the Permanent Joint Council with an enhanced dialogue between the senior military authorities of NATO and its Member States and of Russia.

Ukraine

A similar agreement was signed with Ukraine at the Madrid Summit on 7 July 1997. Given Ukraine's, size, strategic position and recent independence, it was never doubted that Ukraine should also be accorded a special status by NATO.

Following President Kuchma's election victory in 1994, Ukraine had followed a cautious policy towards NATO, joining PfP but remaining neutral on the question of enlargement. But partly as a response to Russian pressure, Ukraine gradually adopted a more pro-NATO stance, welcoming enlargement as a means of enhancing Ukraine's strategic situation.

On 7 July 1997 in Madrid the enhanced bilateral relationship between Ukraine and NATO was sanctioned with the signing of the 'Charter on a Distinctive Partnership between NATO and Ukraine'. The charter specified the principles for the future evolution of NATO–Ukraine relations, the areas and practical aspects of cooperation and consultation, and a general outline of the mutual views on cooperation for a secure Europe.[3]

The Madrid Summit

At the Madrid Summit on 7 July 1997, Poland, the Czech Republic and Hungary were invited to begin accession talks aiming at full NATO membership by the fiftieth anniversary of NATO in April 1999. This decision was taken after a prolonged debate about the criteria for membership (see Enlargement Study) and the number of states which should be invited to join the Alliance.

Those who in early 1997 indicated their desire for membership included Poland, Hungary, the Czech Republic, Romania, Slovenia, Estonia, Latvia, Lithuania, Slovakia, Bulgaria, Albania and the Former Yugoslav Republic of Macedonia (FYROM). In the end it was the US

---

3.   The full text is available on the NATO web site (see Bibliography).

which carried the day, with President Clinton basing his decision on a limited enlargement to three countries as much on internal considerations (Senate ratification) as for any strategic rationale. The US was thus against accession of the Baltic states (as advocated by Denmark) and against the accession of Romania and Slovenia (as advocated by France and Italy). However, due to French and Italian insistence, the final communiqué referred to Romania and Slovenia as aspiring members.[4]

This reference underlined that the limited enlargement by no means excluded the remaining applicants from future membership. NATO stated that it will continue the open door policy vis-á-vis the applicants and that further invitations will be issued in the future, as long as new members 'enhance Euro-Atlantic security and further the principles of the North Atlantic Treaty'. NATO also decided to merge NACC and PfP in a new Euro-Atlantic Partnership Council (EAPC) which aimed to provide an overarching framework for political-military consultations and cooperation in peacekeeping and other activities.

The Madrid Communiqué[5]

> We, the Heads of State and Government of the member countries of the North Atlantic Alliance, have come together in Madrid to give shape to the new NATO as we move towards the 21st century. Substantial progress has been achieved in the internal adaptation of the Alliance. As a significant step in the evolutionary process of opening the Alliance, we have invited three countries to begin accession talks. We have substantially strengthened our relationship with Partners through the new Euro-Atlantic Partnership Council and enhancement of the Partnership for Peace. The signature on 27th May of the NATO–Russia Founding Act and the Charter we will sign tomorrow with Ukraine bear witness to our commitment to an undivided Europe. We are also enhancing our Mediterranean dialogue. Our aim is to reinforce peace and stability in the Euro-Atlantic area.
>
> A new Europe is emerging, a Europe of greater integration and cooperation. An inclusive European security architecture is evolving to which we are contributing, along with other European organizations. Our Alliance will continue to be a driving force in this process.
>
> We are moving towards the realization of our vision of a just and lasting order of peace for Europe as a whole, based on human rights,

4.   See Jonathan Eyal, 'NATO Enlarged; Strategy Correct, Execution Poor', in *International Affairs*, October 1997.
5.   The full text is available on the NATO web site (see Bibliography).

freedom and democracy. In looking forward to the 50th anniversary of the North Atlantic Treaty, we reaffirm our commitment to a strong, dynamic partnership between the European and North American Allies, which has been, and will continue to be, the bedrock of the Alliance and of a free and prosperous Europe. The vitality of the transatlantic link will benefit from the development of a true, balanced partnership in which Europe is taking on greater responsibility. In this spirit, we are building a European Security and Defence Identity within NATO. The Alliance and the European Union share common strategic interests. We welcome the agreements reached at the European Council in Amsterdam. NATO will remain the essential forum for consultation among its members and the venue for agreement on policies bearing on the security and defence commitments of Allies under the Washington Treaty.

While maintaining our core function of collective defence, we have adapted our political and military structures to improve our ability to meet the new challenges of regional crisis and conflict management. NATO's continued contribution to peace in Bosnia and Herzegovina, and the unprecedented scale of cooperation with other countries and international organizations there, reflect the cooperative approach which is key to building our common security. A new NATO is developing: a new NATO for a new and undivided Europe.

The security of NATO's members is inseparably linked to that of the whole of Europe. Improving the security and stability environment for nations in the Euro-Atlantic area where peace is fragile and instability currently prevails remains a major Alliance interest. The consolidation of democratic and free societies on the entire continent, in accordance with OSCE principles, is therefore of direct and material concern to the Alliance. NATO's policy is to build effective cooperation through its outreach activities, including the Euro-Atlantic Partnership Council, with free nations which share the values of the Alliance, including members of the European Union as well as candidates for EU membership.

At our last meeting in Brussels, we said that we would expect and would welcome the accession of new members, as part of an evolutionary process, taking into account political and security developments in the whole of Europe. Twelve European countries have so far requested to join the Alliance. We welcome the aspirations and efforts of these nations. The time has come to start a new phase of this process. The Study on NATO Enlargement—which stated, inter alia, that NATO's military effectiveness should be sustained as the Alliance enlarges—the results of the intensified dialogue with interested Partners, and the analyses of relevant factors associated with the admission of new members have provided a basis on which to assess the current state of preparations of the twelve countries aspiring to Alliance membership.

Today, we invite the Czech Republic, Hungary and Poland to begin accession talks with NATO. Our goal is to sign the Protocol of

Accession at the time of the Ministerial meetings in December 1997 and to see the ratification process completed in time for membership to become effective by the 50th anniversary of the Washington Treaty in April 1999. During the period leading to accession, the Alliance will involve invited countries, to the greatest extent possible and where appropriate, in Alliance activities, to ensure that they are best prepared to undertake the responsibilities and obligations of membership in an enlarged Alliance. We direct the Council in Permanent Session to develop appropriate arrangements for this purpose.

Admitting new members will entail resource implications for the Alliance. It will involve the Alliance providing the resources which enlargement will necessarily require. We direct the Council in Permanent Session to bring to an early conclusion the concrete analysis of the resource implications of the forthcoming enlargement, drawing on the continuing work on military implications. We are confident that, in line with the security environment of the Europe of today, Alliance costs associated with the integration of new members will be manageable and that the resources necessary to meet those costs will be provided.

We reaffirm that NATO remains open to new members under Article 10 of the North Atlantic Treaty. The Alliance will continue to welcome new members in a position to further the principles of the Treaty and contribute to security in the Euro-Atlantic area. The Alliance expects to extend further invitations in coming years to nations willing and able to assume the responsibilities and obligations of membership, and as NATO determines that the inclusion of these nations would serve the overall political and strategic interests of the Alliance and that the inclusion would enhance overall European security and stability... No European democratic country whose admission would fulfil the objectives of the Treaty will be excluded from consideration. Furthermore, in order to enhance overall security and stability in Europe, further steps in the ongoing enlargement process of the Alliance should balance the security concerns of all Allies...

We will review the process at our next meeting in 1999. With regard to the aspiring members, we recognize with great interest and take account of the positive developments towards democracy and the rule of law in a number of south-eastern European countries, especially Romania and Slovenia.

The Alliance recognizes the need to build greater stability, security and regional cooperation in the countries of Southeast Europe, and to promote their increasing integration into the Euro-Atlantic community. At the same time, we recognize the progress achieved towards greater stability and cooperation by the states in the Baltic region which are also aspiring members. As we look to the future of the Alliance, progress towards these objectives will be important for our overall goal of a free, prosperous and undivided Europe at peace.

The establishment of the Euro-Atlantic Partnership Council in Sintra constitutes a new dimension in the relations with our Partners. We look forward to tomorrow's meeting with Heads of State and Government under the aegis of the EAPC.

The Ratification Debate

Once the decision had been taken on the three countries to be invited for accession talks, the debate shifted to the costs and implications of enlargement. The question of the costs of NATO enlargement was left out of the Madrid Declaration, though it mentioned in brief that admitting new members would have resource implications. Prior to the summit there had been widely different estimates of the cost of enlargement. In its 1996 Study the US Congress estimated that the total costs of enlargement would be from 61 to 125 billion dollars,[6] while the RAND Corporation estimated that membership of the 4 Visegrad countries would cost approximately 42 billion over 10 years[7]. The noticeable difference was mainly caused by different assumptions and frameworks for assessing NATO defence requirements. While the Congressional approach was based on the premise of preparing for a resurgent Russian threat, the Rand study was based on avoiding confrontation.

NATO and the US Department of Defense (the Pentagon) divides the costs into three different categories when estimating the total costs of enlargement. The first category is modernization of the new members' armies, including weapons and communication systems, and is estimated to cost between 10 and 13 billion dollars. The second category is the cost of the internal reform and strengthening of NATO, whereas the third represents the cost of ensuring interoperability.

In this respect it is important to point out that the internal modernization, estimated to cost between 8 and 10 billion, is not looked upon as a direct cost of enlargement as it was due in any case. Thus, the actual cost of enlargement is estimated to amount to approximately 20 to 25 billion over the next decade or 15 years. The Pentagon proposes that the new members pay 35 per cent, the Western Europeans pay 50 per cent and the US pays 15 per cent of these expenditures. Thus, empha-

6.   'The Costs of Expanding the NATO Alliance' (Washington DC: Congressional Budget Office, March 1996).

7.   Ronald D. Asmus, Richard L. Kugler and F. Stephen Larrabee, 'What Will NATO Enlargement Cost', *Survival* 38.3 (1996), pp. 27-40.

sizing the low level of threat and the long warning time, the Clinton administration in its first official cost estimate from February this year envisaged a cost of 150 to 200 billion dollars a year for the US during the next 15 years.[8] These costs will mainly be spent improving communications in order to facilitate the new members' participation in NATO operations, rather than strengthening the armed forces.

CFSP/WEU/ESDI

Another aspect of NATO enlargement is the likely impact on EU/WEU efforts to establish a credible Common Foreign and Security Policy (CFSP) and a European Security and Defence Identity (ESDI). According to the Maastricht and Amsterdam Treaties, the CFSP would include the eventual framing of a common defence policy with a central role played by the WEU, the defence alliance established before NATO in 1948, but which has never played a full operational role.

The WEU played a limited role in sanctions monitoring during the Yugoslav conflict and in 1992, at Petersberg near Bonn, the WEU Council of Ministers agreed to strengthen the operational role of the WEU. This implied the Member States providing military units, under WEU authority, which would be employed for peace-keeping, humanitarian and rescue, and peacemaking operations (the Petersberg tasks).

The independent operational ability of carrying out the Petersberg tasks was strengthened at NATO's Brussels Summit in January 1994, when NATO endorsed the possibility of WEU relying on NATO assets for CJTF operations. In order to reflect the emerging ESDI cooperation, consultation and planning procedures between NATO and WEU were improved. At NATO's ministerial meeting in Berlin in June 1996 it was decided to develop the ESDI further within the Alliance, taking full advantage of the combined joint task forces (CJTF) concept. Political control of the Petersberg tasks was devolved to the EU in the Amsterdam Treaty of 1997.

Besides institutional and operational strengthening, WEU has also broadened its geographical scope after the end of the Cold War. In 1991 WEU established a Forum of Consultation with the Central and Eastern European countries and in 1994 Poland, Hungary, the Czech and Slovak Republics, Romania, Bulgaria and the three Baltic states

8. 'The Cost of NATO Expansion? Washington Is Aiming Very Low', *International Herald Tribune* 15 February, 1997.

were given status as associate partners. For non-EU European NATO members (Turkey, Norway and Iceland) WEU offers associate membership, whereas the neutral or ex-neutral countries (Austria, Sweden, Finland and Ireland) and Denmark have observer status. All other EU countries are full members.

Enlargement will provide the Union with more resources to operate the CFSP but at the same time it will mean a more heterogeneous Union and it may become more difficult to agree on common interests as well as decide on how to defend them.

10 |

Conclusion

> The Union's environment is changing fast, both internally and externally. It must set about adapting, developing and reforming itself. Enlargement represents a historic turning point for Europe, an opportunity which it must seize for the sake of its security, its economy, its culture and its status in the world.
>
> Jacques Santer, President of the Commission
> Strasbourg, 16 July 1997

It is quite instructive to look briefly at previous enlargements, which have often been associated with a deepening of the Community. Following the first enlargement involving the UK, Ireland and Denmark, the Community agreed common policies in new areas (e.g. regional, environmental, technology) as well as closer cooperation in foreign affairs (European Political Cooperation [EPC]). Institutional arrangements were also strengthened with the introduction of the European Council and direct elections to the European Parliament.

Following the accession of Greece, and then Spain and Portugal, the Community further developed the structural funds as a mechanism for transfer of resources to the less-developed regions of Member States. This second enlargement wave was also accompanied by the Single European Act, increased involvement of the European Parliament and a new financial resources package for the Community. The Single European Act significantly extended the use of majority voting, without which it would have been impossible to complete the internal market.

The latest enlargement involving Austria, Sweden and finland followed the Treaty on European Union which again involved considerable deepening, for example, the commitment to Economic and Monetary Union, the establishment of a Common Foreign and Security Policy, and yet further powers for the European Parliament.

It is thus quite clear from these examples that enlargement can actually speed up the process of integration, cohesion, and convergence in the Union. With regard to the next enlargement, a deepening of the integration process is even more essential given the number of applicants and the increased diversity their accession will bring to the EU.

The further enlargement of the EU is sometimes presented in negative terms—the cost of taking in poorer members, the difficulty of reforming Union policies, institutional problems, etc. But the potential benefits of enlargement are also considerable because it will:

- enlarge the EU's internal market to include more than 100 million additional consumers with rising incomes;
- support the newly liberalized market economies by further opening up markets in goods and services between east and west, north and south, stimulating economic growth in Europe and offering new trading opportunities for all;
- bind the countries of Central and Eastern Europe into Western European political and economic structures and thus enhance security and stability; both the US (and Russia) support enlargement for this reason;
- increase effective cooperation in the fields of justice and home affairs, helping to fight crime and the menace of drugs, the effects of which are felt throughout our continent;
- bring higher environmental standards to Central and Eastern Europe, benefiting all of Europe by reducing cross-border and global pollution.

The next enlargement is thus an unprecedented historic challenge, requiring imagination and political will of the same order as inspired the foundation of the original European Communities. But unless the EU makes thorough preparations for enlargement, including the functioning and decision-making procedures of the institutions, enlargement could lead to paralysis and even disintegration.

The enlargements which brought Greece, Spain and Portugal into the European Community had as a basic motive the consolidation of democracy and stability in countries which had abandoned totalitarian regimes. For the countries of Central and Eastern Europe, membership of the Union has a similar significance. There can be no question of accepting applicants who do not fulfil the criteria for membership. But assuming they do fulfil the criteria, the efforts required to integrate the applicant countries are well within the capacity of the Union.

If enlargement is to succeed, however, it is essential that it should be well prepared and be accompanied by considerable deepening of the Union. The Union must be able to take decisions quickly and ensure that they are implemented and that they rest on popular support. In effect this means acceptance of a community approach based on the principle of subsidiarity.

But, at the same time, the Union must seek to ensure that further enlargement lives up to the expectations which it has aroused. Candidate countries must be in a position to accept and implement all the rights and obligations which this involves. It is equally important that the Union be in a position to absorb new members, while maintaining its sense of purpose, its integration, and, above all, its capacity to act together in the interests of its citizens.

The prospect of EU membership continues to offer the best incentive to the Central and Eastern Europeans to persevere with political and economic transformation. The changes which have to be made are often painful, and so far have brought little reward for politicians in office. Without the sustained encouragement of the EU, a number of countries could easily be blown off course.

It is clear, therefore, that there is much work ahead for the associated countries and the Union in preparing for enlargement. But instead of feeling impatient at the time needed to complete this process, it is important to seize the opportunity offered by the next years to make a real success of the preaccession strategy. The more that can be achieved in advance, the easier the accession negotiations will be.

No one can predict how long these negotiations will last. Both Chancellor Kohl and President Chirac have mentioned the year 2000 as a target date for membership. The financial proposals in Agenda 2000 assume that some countries will join in 2002. Some commentators have suggested that even this is too optimistic a date for membership, given the complexities of the negotiating process.

Regardless of the date of accession, the Union is now embarked on a historic mission to unite the continent. The division of Europe which persisted for more than a generation after the Second World War was entirely artificial. It corresponded to no traditional distinction of politics, religion or culture, and it made no sense in terms of geography or economics. The next enlargement thus presents enormous challenges and possibilities; it will change the map of Europe, and it will change the political and economic composition of the European Union. Europe's political leaders, in east and west, will have to display a blend of statesmanship and creativity, idealism and realism to rise to this challenge and satisfy the aspirations of the European peoples for a wider and stronger Union.

Appendix 1

Chronology

20 March 1985	Mikhail Gorbachev is appointed Secretary General of the Communist Party of the Soviet Union.
2 May 1989	Hungary cuts the first hole in the Iron Curtain. By 11 September all borders will be open. Mass exodus of citizens from the GDR starts.
17 July 1989	Austria applies for membership of the EC.
24 August 1989	Following Solidarity's victory in the 4 June elections in Poland, Tadeusz Mazowiecki becomes the first non-Communist prime minister in the Eastern bloc.
9 November 1989	Fall of the Berlin Wall.
29 November 1989	'Velvet revolution' in Czechoslovakia.
22 December 1989	The Romanian army joins the demonstrating opposition and overthrows Nicolae Ceaucescu, who is executed three days later.
11 March 1990	Lithuania declares full independence.
30 March 1990	Estonia declares full independence.
1 July 1990	German economic and monetary union—de facto reunification.
4 July 1990	Cyprus applies for membership of EC; Malta applies a few days later on 16 July.
6 July 1990	NATO leaders release the London Declaration declaring that the two blocs no longer consider each other adversaries and that NATO will revise its strategy.
28 July 1990	Latvia declares full independence.
3 October 1990	Formal reunification of Germany.
1 July 1991	Sweden applies for membership of EC.
19 August 1991	Coup attempt by Soviet hardliners fails. Gorbachev returns to Moscow, where Russian President Boris Yeltsin is his new challenger aiming at dismantling the Soviet Union.
10 December 1991	European Council at Maastricht agrees the Maastricht Treaty that lays down the timetable for economic and monetary union, provides for a new security and

	defence dimension to EC cooperation, and creates the European Union.
31 December 1991	Following Ukraine's declaration of independence and the Minsk agreement, the Soviet Union ceases to exist. The flag of the Russian Federation is raised over the Kremlin.
18 March 1992	Finland applies for membership of EU.
25 November 1992	Norway applies for membership of EU.
12 December 1992	European Council at Edinburgh welcomes the Commissions report *Towards a Closer Association with the Countries of Central and Eastern Europe*, focused on enhanced political dialogue and increased market access.
1 January 1993	Czechoslovakia splits up into two independent states— the Czech Republic and Slovakia.
22 June 1993	European Council at Copenhagen decides that the associated CEECs which so wish could become members of the European Union as soon as they were able to fulfil the relevant criteria.
1 November 1993	The Maastricht Treaty comes into force.
11 December 1993	European Council at Brussels supports the idea of the Stability Pact for Central and Eastern Europe, aiming at averting tension and conflicts, consolidating borders and resolving problems of national minorities—also called the *Balladur Plan.*
January 1994	NATO Summit at Brussels invites all democratic countries in Europe to join Partnership for Peace (PfP).
1 February 1994	Europe Agreements signed with Poland and Hungary.
25 June 1994	European Council in Corfu: signature of Treaty of Accession with Austria, Sweden, Finland and Norway. Notes 'that the next phase of enlargement will involve Cyprus and Malta'.
10 December 1994	European Council in Essen agrees comprehensive preaccession strategy proposed by the Commission. Also requests Commission to prepare further reports on the impact of enlargement on the Union, and to submit a White Paper on the CEECs and the internal market. Also agrees 'that the institutional conditions for ensuring the proper functioning of the Union must be created at the 1996 Intergovernmental Conference, which for that reason must take place before accession negotiations begin'.
1 January 1995	Austria, Finland and Sweden join the EU.
1 February 1995	Europe Agreements with Bulgaria, Romania, the Czech Republic and Slovakia.

21 March 1995	The Stability Pact is signed in Paris. The signatories entrust to the CSCE the monitoring of bilateral agreements, and set up projects for regional boundary cooperation, minority issues, cultural cooperation and environmental problems.
12 June 1995	Europe Agreements signed with Estonia, Latvia and Lithuania.
27 June 1995	European Council in Cannes invites CEEC heads of government to participate in part of the meeting. Reaffirmed that negotiations with Cyprus and Malta would begin six months after the conclusion of the IGC.
September 1995	NATO publishes the Enlargement Study, which puts enlargement back on track.
16 December 1995	European Council in Madrid requested Commission 'to expedite preparation of its opinions on the applications made so that they can be forwarded to the Council as soon as possible after the conclusion of the Intergovernmental Conference. The European Council hopes that the preliminary stage of negotiations will coincide with the start of negotiations with Cyprus and Malta.'
31 March 1996	Opening of the Intergovernmental Conference (IGC) in Turin.
6 June 1996	Europe Agreement signed with Slovenia.
22 June 1996	The European Council in florence simply reiterates the conclusions of Madrid concerning enlargement.
14 December 1996	The European Council in Dublin welcome the Commission's intentions to present proposals for an overall reinforcement of the preaccession strategy together with its opinions and other reports.
22 May 1997	NATO and Russia sign the Founding Act on Mutual Relations, which launches the Permanent Joint Council.
17 June 1997	European Council at Amsterdam agrees the Amsterdam Treaty. Accession negotiations should start with individual countries 'according to the stage which is reached in satisfying the basic conditions of membership and in preparing for accession'.
7 July 1997	NATO Summit in Madrid invites Poland, the Czech Republic and Hungary to begin accession talks aiming at membership in 1999.
16 July 1997	Commission publishes 'Agenda 2000' including plans for future financing of the EU after 1999, reforms of agricultural policy and structural funds, and a strategy for enlargement of the EU, together with the ten Opinions on the applicants for membership of the EU.

December 1997   European Council in Luxembourg endorses Commission recommendations to open accession negotiations with the five CEECs and Cyprus; agrees to establish accession patnerships with all 11 candidates.

Appendix 2

The Future European Union

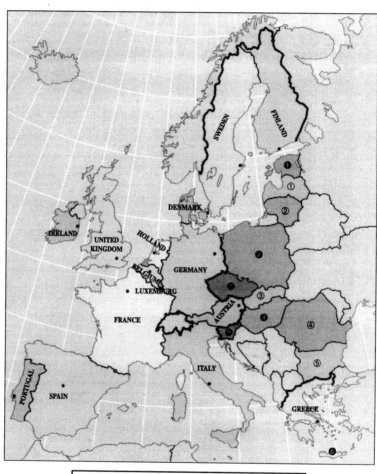

Fast Track Applicants:	Other Applicants:
❶ Estonia	① Latvia
❷ Poland	② Lithuania
❸ Czech Republic	③ Slovakia
❹ Hungary	④ Romania
❺ Slovenia	⑤ Bulgaria
❻ Cyprus	

Appendix 3

Tables

Table 1: Overview of the new financial framework 2000–2006 (1997 prices)

ecu billion—1997 prices— Appropriation for commitments	1999	2000	2001	2002	2003	2004	2005	2006
Agriculture (guideline)	**43.3**	**44.1**	**45.0**	**46.1**	**47.0**	**48.0**	**49.0**	**50.0**
Structural Operations	**36.1**	**35.2**	**36.0**	**38.8**	**39.8**	**40.7**	**41.7**	**42.8**
of which: past adjustments	*1.8*							
Internal Policies	**6.1**	**6.1**	**6.4**	**7.3**	**7.5**	**7.7**	**7.9**	**8.1**
External Action	**6.6**	**6.6**	**6.8**	**7.0**	**7.1**	**7.3**	**7.5**	**7.6**
Administration	**4.5**	**4.5**	**4.6**	**5.1**	**5.2**	**5.3**	**5.4**	**5.5**
Reserves	**1.2**	**1.0**	**1.0**	**0.8**	**0.5**	**0.5**	**0.5**	**0.5**
Appropriations for commitments —Total	**97.8**	**97.5**	**99.8**	**105.1**	**107.1**	**109.5**	**112.0**	**114.5**
Appropriations for payments —Total	**92.5**	**94.1**	**96.6**	**101.1**	**103.9**	**106.5**	**108.9**	**111.4**
Appropriations for payments (as percentage of GNP)	1.25	1.24	1.24	1.22	1.22	1.22	1.22	1.22
Margin	0.02	0.03	0.03	0.05	0.05	0.05	0.05	0.05
Own resources ceiling	**1.27**	**1.27**	**1.27**	**1.27**	**1.27**	**1.27**	**1.27**	**1.27**
Internal policies if growth at same rate as total GNP	6.132	6.285	6.442	6.856	7.031	7.211	7.395	7.584
External action if growth at same rate as total GNP	6.596	6.761	6.930	7.375	7.563	7.756	7.955	8.158
Administration if growth at same rate as total GNP	4.535	4.648	4.765	5.070	5.200	5.333	5.469	5.609
Internal Policies	**6.132**	**6.132**	**6.442**	**7.303**	**7.493**	**7.687**	**7.886**	**8.089**
External Action	**6.596**	**6.596**	**6.796**	**6.955**	**7.119**	**7.287**	**7.461**	**7.640**
Administration	**4.535**	**4.535**	**4.617**	**5.060**	**5.185**	**5.322**	**5.410**	**5.500**

Table 2: Heading 1: Agricultural expenditure (current prices

ecu billion	1999	2000	2001	2002	2003	2004	2005	2006
Guideline (current prices)[1]	**45.0**	**46.7**	**48.5**	**50.6**	**52.6**	**54.7**	**56.9**	**59.2**
Agricultural expenditure (current prices)	—	**44.0**	**45.9**	**49.7**	**52.1**	**53.2**	**53.9**	**54.5**
Community of 15								
Reformed CAP	41.7	41.6	43.4	45.4	47.3	47.9	47.9	47.9
New rural development accompanying measures and horizontal fisheries measures		1.9	2.0	2.0	2.0	2.0	2.1	2.1
New Member States								
CAP (market measures)		0.0	0.0	1.1	1.2	1.2	1.3	1.4
Specific rural development accompanying measures		0.0	0.0	0.6	1.0	1.5	2.0	2.5
Preaccession aid[2]		0.5	0.5	0.6	0.6	0.6	0.6	0.6
Margin		*2.7*	*2.6*	*0.9*	*0.5*	*1.5*	*3.0*	*4.7*

1. Assumed 2% deflator per year from 1999 to 2006.
2. Equal to ecu 500 million at constant 1997 prices.

Table 3: Heading 2: Expenditure on structural operations

ecu billion (1997 prices)	1999	2000	2001	2002	2003	2004	2005	2006
Community of fifteen								
Structural Funds	31.4	31.3	32.1	31.3	30.3	29.2	28.2	27.3
Cohesion Fund	2.9	2.9	2.9	2.9	2.9	2.9	2.9	2.9
New Member States[1]		0.0	0.0	3.6	5.6	7.6	9.6	11.6
Preaccession aid		1.0	1.0	1.0	1.0	1.0	1.0	1.0
TOTAL	34.3	35.2	36.0	38.8	39.8	40.7	41.7	42.8

1. Including participation in the Cohesion Fund.

Table 4: Pre-accession aid and expenditure with the accession of new Member States

ecu billion (1997 prices)	1999	2000	2001	2002	2003	2004	2005	2006
TOTAL PREACCESSION AID	**1.3**	**3.0**	**3.0**	**3.0**	**3.0**	**3.0**	**3.0**	**3.0**
Heading 1		0.5	0.5	0.5	0.5	0.5	0.5	0.5
Heading 2		1.0	1.0	1.0	1.0	1.0	1.0	1.0
Heading 4[1]	1.3	1.5	1.5	1.5	1.5	1.5	1.5	1.5
Other applicant countries[2]	0.5	1.2	1.2	3.0	3.0	3.0	3.0	3.0
New Member States[2]	*0.8*	*1.8*	*1.8*					
Amounts for the New Member States				**5.8**	**8.2**	**10.8**	**13.3**	**15.7**
Heading 1[3]				1.5	1.9	2.4	2.9	3.3
Heading 2				3.6	5.6	7.6	9.6	11.6
Heading 3				0.7	0.7	0.8	0.8	0.8

1. The 1999 amount is intended as a guide.
2. The breakdown for 1999 to 2001 is purely indicative.
3. Figures converted to 1997 prices for purposes of comparison. Only the estimates in current prices are relevant

Expenditure in Categories 3, 4 and 5
(billion ecu, 1997 prices)

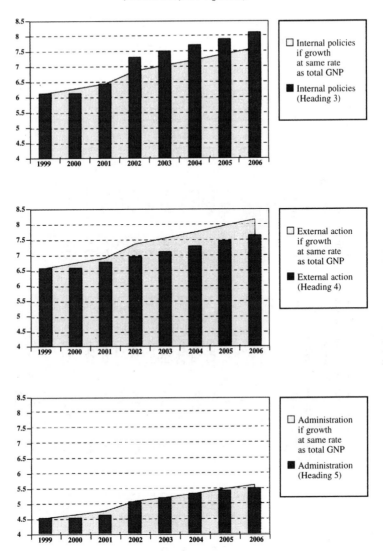

Applicant Countries of Central and Eastern Europe and EU Member States
Basic Data (Year 1995)

	Area	Population		GDP at current market prices			GDP at purchasing power standards			Agriculture	
	(1000 km²)	(millions)	density (inh/km²)	(billion ecu)	(in ecu per head)	(in ecu per head as % of EU average)	(billion ecu)	(in ecu per head at PPP rates)	(in ecu per head as % of EU average)	(% of total gross value added)	(% of empl.)
	1	2	3	4	5	6	7	8	9	10	11
Hungary	93	10.2	110	33.4	3340	19	64.6	6310	37	6.2	8.0
Poland	313	38.6	123	90.2	2360	14	203.3	5320	31	7.6	26.9
Romania	238	22.7	95	27.3	1200	7	94.3	4060	23	20.5	34.4
Slovak Rep.	49	5.4	110	13.3	2470	14	38.0	7120	41	6.3	9.7
Latvia	65	2.5	38	3.4	1370	8	7.9	3160	18	9.9	18.5
Estonia	45	1.5	33	2.8	1850	11	5.9	3920	23	8.1	13.1
Lithuania	65	3.7	57	3.5	930	5	15.3	4130	24	9.3	23.8
Bulgaria	111	8.4	76	9.9	1180	7	35.4	4210	24	13.9	23.2*
Czech Rep.	79	10.3	130	36.1	3490	20	97.2	9410	55	5.2	6.3
Slovenia	20	2.0	100	14.2	7240	42	20.1	10110	59	5.0	7.1
CE 10	1078	105.3	98	234	2220	13	582.0	5530	32	8.6	22.5
—in % of EU 15	33	28	85	4	13		9	32		358	425

	1	2	3	4	5	6	7	8	9	10	11
Belgium	31	10.1	332	205.9	20310	118	196.0	19340	112	1.7*	2.7
Denmark	43	5.2	121	132.1	25260	146	104.4	19960	116	3.7*	4.4
Germany	357	81.5	228	1845.2	22600	131	1556.8	19070	110	1.0*	3.2
Greece	132	10.4	79	87.4	8360	48	118.4	11320	66	14.7*	20.4
Spain	506	39.2	77	428.1	10920	63	518.8	13230	77	3.7*	9.3
France	544	58.0	107	1174.3	20200	117	1076.5	18520	107	2.5*	4.9
Ireland	70	3.6	51	49.2	13740	80	57.4	16020	93	7.5*	12.0
Italy	301	57.3	190	831.4	14250	83	1036.8	1770	103	2.9*	7.5
Luxembourg	3	0.4	157	13.3	32370	187	11.9	29140	169	1.5*	3.9
Netherlands	42	15.4	371	302.5	19570	113	284.3	18390	107	3.6*	3.8
Austria	84	8.0	96	178.4	22180	128	155.5	19320	112	2.4*	7.3
Portugal	92	9.9	108	77.1	7770	45	115.2	11620	67	5.1*	11.5
Finland	338	5.1	15	95.6	18720	108	84.5	16550	96	5.2*	7.8
Sweden	450	8.8	20	176.3	19970	116	153.5	17390	101	2.1*	3.3
UK	244	58.5	240	844.8	14410	83	971.7	16580	96	1.6*	2.1
EU 15	3 236	371.6	115	6441.5	17260	100	6441.5	17260	100	2.4*	5.3

* 1994

Sources: CEECs: Col. 1–10: Eurostat, based on data from the CEEC Statistical Institutes
Col. 11: Statistical Yearbooks from the CEEC Statistical Institutes
EU Member States: Eurostat

Notes: Exact compatibility of CEEC Statistical Institutes date with EU standards on statistics and thus the compatibility with EU figures can still not be guaranteed. Major changes to these data are still possible.
For calculating the per capita GDP data, the populations according to national account definition are used. Purchasing power parity (PPP) exchange rates are commonly used in place of official exchange rates to estimate relative standards of living. They therefore take into account cost differences between countries.

EURIS Trade with CEECs: January–June 1997

	January–June 1997			J–J 1996	Year 1996		
	MECU	growth rate J–J 97/J–J 96 %	exp./imp. %	MECU	MECU	Growth rate 1996/1995 %	exp./imp. %
10 CEEC							
EU exp.	36534	21	138	30129	63540	19	135
EU imp.	26552	16		22808	47071	6	
Balance	9982			7321	16469		
5 CEEC[1]							
EU exp.	29579	23	145	24097	50896	20	141
EU imp.	20450	16		17549	36178	6	
Balance	9129			6548	14718		
Poland							
EU exp.	11739	30	173	9026	19793	31	162
EU imp.	6792	14		5933	12218	-1	
Balance	4947			3093	7575		
Hungary							
EU exp.	6084	29	116	4715	9902	14	114
EU imp.	5266	26		4162	8708	15	
Balance	818			553	1194		
Czech Rep.							
EU exp.	7685	14	141	6708	13909	20	143
EU imp.	5433	14		4747	9694	8	
Balance	2252			1961	4215		
Slovakia							
EU exp.	2346	24	123	1884	3964	24	117
EU imp.	1902	13		1688	3386	10	
Balance	444			196	578		